ACKNOWLEDGMENTS

In Preparation: Particular thanks to Jot. help and support of and during the 'preparation walk'

For the Inspiration: Thanks to the many people who campaigned for the right to roam the countryside over many years and in particular for those whose brainchild the Pennine Way was. Journalist and rambler Tom Stephenson first proposed the concept in an article in the Daily Herald in 1935. He subsequently campaigned for parliament to adopt the official trail. He had been inspired by similar long distance routes in the USA; in particular the Appalachian Trail. Thanks also to the many people who have written about the Pennine Way since, a number of whose accounts led me to want to join their number.

During the walk: Special thanks to Maureen, Martin and Trevor who all 'signed up' in advance to share a part of the journey with me. Thanks too for those fellow Pennine Way walkers who became very much a part of my journey; Paul and Trevor, Dave, Gary, Susan, Arthur, Con, Julie and others whose 'journeys' crossed my own, but for whom I do not have a name. Thanks to Sandra for picking me up at Bradford Interchange on Day Two and to Christine for dropping off Trevor at Twice Brewed and for relieving me of my tent, sleeping bag, mat and several maps on Day Eleven. Thanks to Rob for shortening and making easier the first leg of the trip home from Kirk Yetholm to Berwick. Thank you too to my 'daily blog followers' for their encouraging and supportive responses.

Staff and Trustees of DAB: A big thank you to all the staff, trustees and volunteers who helped in creating and establishing the 'ALL ALOUD' singers, in particular; Martin, Lis, Jenny, Joyce, Jennifer, Mark, Myra, Kathryn, Sue, Angela Janet and Mark.

In writing and creating this book: A very big thank you to Margot, Martin and Sue W for their critical yet constructive advice and support in relation to the book itself and to Mark, Julie, Gary, Sue W and many others in relation to its' publication. Thank you too to Sue C and all at Bradford Talking Media (BTM) for enabling the creation of an audio version of the book.

For their support throughout 'my journey': Thank you to all those of you who have given or pledged your financial support to the development of ALL ALOUD and who purchase this book in the certain knowledge that in so doing you are securing its long term sustainability.

Finally no journey of this kind and the opportunity to undertake it would have been possible without the support of family. Sandra has been a source of great support for almost forty years and together with my daughters, Becky and Jenny encouraged me in my quest. Finally to my grand-daughter Bella, who has inspired me in so many ways since she became a part of my life two years ago.

Printed by Inprint & Design, Bradford
www.inprintdesign.com

CONTENTS

CHAPTER 1: THE PREPARATION WALK — Page 1

CHAPTER 2: TRAVEL TO EDALE — Page 16

CHAPTER 3: DAY ONE – EDALE TO CROWDEN — Page 24

CHAPTER 4: DAY TWO – CROWDEN TO HOME! — Page 31

CHAPTER 5: HOME TO BLACKSHAW HEAD — Page 45

CHAPTER 6: BLACKSHAW HEAD TO COWLING — Page 49

CHAPTER 7: COWLING TO ABOVE MALHAM TARN — Page 57

CHAPTER 8: ABOVE MALHAM TARN TO HAWES — Page 64

CHAPTER 9: HAWES TO TAN HILL — Page 73

CHAPTER 10: TAN HILL TO MIDDLETON-IN-TEESDALE — Page 81

CHAPTER 11: MIDDLETON-IN-TEESDALE TO DUFTON — Page 88

CHAPTER 12: DUFTON TO GARRIGILL — Page 95

CHAPTER 13: GARRIGILL TO TWICE BREWED — Page 106

CHAPTER 14: TWICE BREWED TO BELLINGHAM — Page 116

CHAPTER 15: BELLINGHAM TO BYRNESS — Page 124

CHAPTER 16: BYRNESS TO KIRK YETHOLM — Page 137

CHAPTER 17: KIRK YETHOLM TO HOME — Page 144

GUIDE BOOKS AND MAPS USED — Page 148

PLACES I STAYED IN DURING MY PENNINE WAY JOURNEY — Page 149

SUMMITS (OVER 400Metres) I VISITED DURING MY JOURNEY — Page 152

To Margot

Thanks again for all your help
Enjoy the re-read

Peter

CHAPTER ONE

The preparation walk: Cleveland Way from Helmsley to Saltburn

Together with a small group of friends and similarly like minded individuals a number of years ago the 'Challenge Committee' was born. At that time we all worked together and enjoyed fell walking and wanted to block out one or two long weekends a year to embark upon a 'walking challenge'. Having together climbed the national three Peaks within 24 hours, the Lyke Wake Walk within 24 hours, completed the Dales Way, undertaken a number of Lake District walks and climbed in Arran, in 2011 the 'committee' completed in two days the coastal section of the Cleveland Way from Saltburn to Scarborough, a distance of some 44 miles. What better preparation for my Pennine Way journey than to undertake the Helmsley to Saltburn Section?

I had long held an ambition to walk the Pennine Way, from reading early accounts of its creation, to stories about those who had taken on the challenge. I am never happier than when out in the great outdoors and whilst I enjoy the company of others I can also enjoy my own company and feel connected to the landscape, when walking the hills. The prospect of walking from the Peak District in Derbyshire, up and over the Pennines, taking in the Yorkshire Dales, the high Cumbrian Pennine Fells, finishing with the Cheviots in Northumberland and finally arriving in Scotland, was an adventure I longed to have, but one that required a minimum of two weeks availability to undertake. Finally in the summer of 2012 that opportunity arose for me.

Whilst I had enjoyed walking, particularly in the Lakeland fells, for many years and had undertaken some long distance walks, the Pennine Way would be my longest continuous walk by a long way, both in terms of days walked (seven days was my previous limit) and in terms of the distance covered. It would be almost three times as long as my previous longest continuous distance. Despite the fact that I was reasonably fit and active, I didn't know whether I would stay the distance. I definitely needed a walk to test as far as I could my ability to walk in excess of 20 miles a day with a rucksack containing all that I would need for such a journey.

I had retired early from my role as a Senior Manager in Adult Social Care in 2009, following over forty years Local Government service with three Authorities; all but two of the forty years were spent in the field of Social Services. I had then worked as a self-employed Social Care Consultant and since retirement had used my previous experience and skills to support three local organisations on a voluntary basis. My fellow 'Challenge Committee' members were all however still at work.

So being the only retired member of the Challenge Committee, I had also agreed to fulfil the role of 'social secretary'. This effectively meant getting other members to agree to Challenge activity dates and to specific Challenge activities. Once agreed, which usually took some doing, it also meant finding and booking any accommodation required and sorting out travel arrangements.

In April 2012 I had managed to get confirmation from both John and Simon that they were both available from Friday 29th June to Sunday 1st July and that they were keen to walk the first section of the Cleveland Way, finishing in Saltburn. John and I had been friends for around 25 years and had shared a lot together. We both hailed from the same town, supported the same football team, worked together until my retirement for the same Local Authority, lived within a quarter of a mile of each other and had children of a similar age. John and I had walked many a mile together over the years. John also introduced me to running, a past time I didn't take up until I was 49. I had subsequently gone on to run 12 marathons and encouraged and supported John to complete his first (my eleventh) marathon in Venice in 2010. Simon had worked with John and me for around 20 years. His work involved Health and Safety and latterly Human Resources more generally.

He was the youngest of our 'Committee' and as such his children were much younger too. I had provided advice to Simon when he had decided to take up running and he had enjoyed completing his first marathon in 2009. He had decided to enter the Edinburgh marathon in May 2012 and I didn't need a lot of persuasion to come out of my self-imposed marathon retirement to agree to run with him. We had enjoyed running together, despite it being the hottest ever Edinburgh marathon and had both completed the run in around four hours.

So it was that two and a half weeks before the start of my Pennine Way adventure, I set off early one Friday morning on my training walk linking up with John and Simon. I was using the walk to test as much as possible some recently acquired equipment; 65 litre rucksack, lightweight cagoule; and to carry the weight I would have with me when undertaking the Pennine Way. Given that we planned to cover the 60 miles of the Cleveland Way, from Helmsley to Saltburn by 3pm on the third day and be home in time to watch the European Championship Cup Final, my pack did somewhat dwarf the weekend sacks of my compatriots.

I left home at 6.25am and by half past was at John's, for the mile or so walk down to Saltaire station to catch the train to Leeds, where we would link up with Simon. The day was dry, thus far, though the previous two days had seen flash flooding in parts of the UK, not for the first time during this wet summer. At Leeds we boarded the 7.10am train to York; an Edinburgh bound train that would, because of the floods, only go as far as Newcastle today. This was certainly going to present a challenge to an excited and giggly 'hen party' group of about a dozen girls who were off to Edinburgh for the weekend and who shared our carriage.

Once at York we had about a 15 minute walk to a small bus terminus in Exhibition Square, described in some guidebooks as the prettiest bus stop in the UK. It was indeed very pleasant with its island beds of flowers and its little square set amongst historic buildings. Before long our bus to Helmsley arrived and for an hour and twenty minutes transported us through some delightful countryside. During our journey we were three of only five paying passengers, one for the first fifteen minutes and the second from Ampleforth to Helmsley. The bus did however also double as the school run to Easingwold High School, so for a short time we also had the company of about twenty or so youngsters and their 'chatter'. After they had disembarked we carried on to the square in the centre of Easingwold and stopped whilst our driver, to our amazement and amusement, delivered a vacuum cleaner to a local resident who was clearly expecting it. On the next leg of our journey we caught sight of the White Horse at Sutton Bank, where we would hope to be by lunch time.

We arrived at the picturesque market town of Helmsley, the starting point for the Cleveland Way and we visited the facilities there and I introduced John and Simon to the delights of the local delicatessen/pie shop. We had a very pleasant morning walk before arriving at the Hambleton Inn, just before Sutton Bank, where we caused many a raised eyebrow by ordering a pot of tea (instead of a beer) and sitting outside on a picnic bench enjoying our first 'rest' of the day. Once at Sutton Bank the views were spectacular as our route took us along the escarpment top. However, after a little while we could see some rain approaching from the west and before long we were experiencing our first, and what turned out to be the only, shower of the day. It was heavy at times and lasted for half an hour but fully tested the waterproofness of the new cagoule.

Finally leaving the escarpment, although still with fine long distance views to the west we arrived at a spot between a deserted stone house to our right, protected from the prevailing wind by a small cluster of trees to our left. The only sound was of the breeze blowing through the trees, a perfect place to stop for a short while for a drink of water and a quick bite to eat. About a mile further on we emerged on to a metalled track that bends down and out of sight to our left and rises steeply to our right. As we head upwards a large black and tan dog which, as we get to know her better, appears to be a cross between a Rottweiler and a

Doberman, walks up from the left to 'greet' us. The road climbs and climbs and as we become aware that our footsteps are being 'dogged' by our four legged friend, eventually starts to level out at a farm. Here another dog emerges from our right, to meet us, or hopefully to meet her fellow canine paramour.

However as we leave the farm and turn right along a grassy track with large tractor tracks either side, we are surprised to find our doggy friend still in tow. After a while we come to a gate and manoeuvre the three of us through it whilst leaving our friendly mutt on the other side. Walking onwards feeling pleased with ourselves we then hear the rattle of metal as our doggy friend scrambles between the bars of the gate and continues her 'love affair' with our heels. It is clear that although she is an old dog she has recently had a litter of pups too. She also has a rather large growth on one flank. Surely she either knows where she is going or will soon return 'home'. We arrive at another gate, where the bars are even closer together, and again ensure we are through and away, but as before she manages to scramble through and rejoins us.

We are now starting to imagine she will be with us all the way to Osmotherley and to discuss what we can do to 'lose' her before then. A gate appears to our left, which leads to a path going diagonally back in the general direction we have come and we coax our four legged friend through, before closing the gate. We plead with her to go home like a good girl and head off. Yet again our persistent and 'loyal' follower negotiates the gate and rejoins us.

Ahead in the distance we see something that is bright red in colour and try to work out what it is. Is it a person in a bright red cagoule, is it a car, is it a piece of farm machinery? Soon we are aware of another 'red object' further beyond it too. Our 'companion', for I think that her efforts to remain with us now at least grant her that status, remains steadfastly in tune with our pace, which has quickened as we try to resolve the mystery of the red blobs ahead. She has now been with us for about 90 minutes or 4 miles and whilst she is clearly not in her prime, shows no signs of giving up on her 'quest'. Our grassy track also continues and efforts have been made to fill in some of the tractor ruts on either side to ensure the 'route' is passable in an appropriate off road vehicle. The moorland around us is clearly grouse territory and we surmise the 'improvements' to the track must relate to this.

We suddenly realise that before the first of our red blobs, which by now we can tell are clearly not people and are too big to be cars, is a white van, which as we approach, reveals itself to have an occupant with a spaniel. We ask him whether he has any knowledge of to whom or where our companion might belong. He is waiting for a group of young 'Princes Trust' walkers and whilst he doesn't offer to directly help us with our doggy dilemma, does tell us that if we find the 'gamekeeper' who should be working further ahead, he may be able to help us.

Finally it becomes clear that our red blobs are in fact diggers with gravel/stones in their broad serrated 'buckets'. There are two men in attendance, one driving and manoeuvring the digger to tip sufficient stones into any potholes, the other using a spade to spread these as evenly as possible to cover the ruts and to guide the driver to the right spots. We explain our doggy dilemma again and neither recognises our companion, however we are assured that the 'gamekeeper' is working at/on the next red digger ahead and that he will take the dog off our hands and resolve matters.

After about 10 minutes we arrive at the next digger to be greeted by the perfect conversation opener, "You should have that dog on a lead". This gives us the opportunity to plead for mercy and enquire whether it is the gamekeeper himself to whom we are talking. It turns out to be the driver of our second red blob who is the gamekeeper and having appraised himself of the situation, he asserts that his companion will hang on to the dog whilst he retrieves his phone from his 4x4 parked about 400metres away and makes the necessary enquiries. Our doggy story is finally at an end.

The gamekeepers' companion makes a fuss of the dog, something we have steadfastly refused to do for the past two hours, and hangs on to her. We gleefully carry on, feeling relieved of 'our burden' at last. Obviously the next two hours are spent in reproachful and remorseful conversation, as our concern for the welfare and wellbeing of our companion grows and we wonder whether her story will have a happy outcome.

We now enjoy a pleasant walk down into Osmotherley, where we are booked into the Queen Catherine Hotel. We dine there, but also visit the other two pubs that are on different sides of the triangular green that is the centre point of the village. We have covered 22miles today and the equipment stood up well. I discovered later on however that I had had the rucksack too tight on the hips, so both my sides above the hip bone had chafed and were red and a little sore. A slight adjustment to the straps resolved this for the remainder of the walk and by the time I got home the redness had faded. We had also sat straight down on finishing the days' walk, which resulted in a little stiffness, so resolved to do some warm down exercise at the end of the next day.

The first part of our walk on the Saturday from Osmotherley to Great Ayton retraced the steps of the Lyke Wake Walk, (The Challenge Committees' least favourite walking experience of all time) although this time the more scenic bit of that route was covered in day light.

The 42 miles of the Lyke Wake walk had involved two vehicles and a continuous walk commencing at 8.30pm. We had all driven to Ravenscar to ditch my vehicle there and then driven back in John's car to leave it at the starting point. Setting off as dusk approached we had made a wrong turning after two miles which had resulted in us having to back track for a mile. It was dark therefore whilst we were covering the Section of the route we would coincide with today.

We met a Canadian couple who were walking the Coast to Coast route and realised that the Cleveland way also embraces part of this route too for a while. We hadn't ordered a packed lunch, I had plenty of snacks, dried apricots, yoghurt coated raisins, apple bars, biscuits and anyway according to the guide book we were following there was a cafe at a car park, just off our route, where we should arrive at about 12 .30pm.

Whilst John and Simon were contemplating what kind of sandwiches may be on offer as we approached the car-park, I was mulling over what from my 'larder' I would dine on. It turns out that the cafe, which apparently and ironically was very popular, closed about 18months ago and so my extensive larder is shared to supplement snacks that John and Simon have with them too. We de-boot and engage in some gentle exercises and stretching. A pleasant break in the sunshine is enjoyed before we set off again.

We arrive at the Wainstones, a distinctive rock outcrop at the western end of Hasty Bank and are rewarded with some wonderful views of the Tees Valley to the North. Our walk now enables a greater understanding of the history of the area as we pass and encounter evidence of Bronze Age burial grounds, way markers and boundary stones that have stood for hundreds of years and of more recent mining activity. Just prior to leaving the Lyke Wake Way route and swinging round to follow the ridges of the moorland hills, the sky turns black and we are hit by a short (fifteen minutes) but squally and heavy shower of rain and hailstones, so the rain-cover of the rucksack and the waterproofs are again put to the test. As the storm dies away we are able now to look back over our route and the long distance views across the weather plain to the west. Looking ahead we can see the distinctive summit of Roseberry Topping.

Six years ago on the Lyke Wake Walk it was just starting to get light at this point. The route then followed a seemingly endless trek across featureless moor-land, with everyone else apart from me getting blisters. When we finally arrived at Ravenscar at 4pm we were weary, tired and foot sore. I then had to drive us back to link up with John's car, before we drove in convoy to Whitby, where we were staying for the night. We got there at 7pm and I remember having to be shaken by my

compatriots to stop me falling asleep over my meal in the pub that night.

We drop down into Rydale, which is a collection of dwellings, including a church and a café; which of course is closed by this time. Rydale also has a railway station, as it straddles the Esk Valley line that runs from Middlesbrough to Whitby. I use the opportunity of a public telephone box to ring the landlady of the B&B we are staying in tonight to inform her of our 'E.T.A.'. Just as well as there is no mobile signal here.

As we head out of Rydale the rain arrives again and for the remainder of our walk to Great Ayton is our constant companion. It is a steep pull up a metalled road and then through a forested area to the Captain Cook monument and then we drop down to another road, where we leave the Cleveland Way in order to find our B&B in Great Ayton. The day has involved a long 24 mile walk, not without incident, which we relive over a pint and a meal in the Royal Oak.

The Sunday dawned cooler but dry and bright as we headed back to rejoin the Cleveland Way and climbed up to Roseberry Topping, before heading east to the coast at Saltburn. It was a pleasant country walk and we enjoyed our brief lunch stop at a pub after about 9 miles. After this the scenery changed as we walked down farm tracks and through more urban landscapes as we neared the coast. We arrived in Saltburn in time for tea and cake before our train home was due to depart.

The train journey involved two changes, the first at Darlington and the second at Leeds. Ironically Sandra, my wife, was travelling up to the North East on that day and after several texts back and forth, I realised that we had a half hour wait at Darlington and that her train to Newcastle was due to stop at Darlington during this 'window'. She informed me of the carriage she was in and I was on the platform when the Newcastle train pulled in. We exchanged a kiss in the doorway of her carriage before she sped northwards and I rejoined John and Simon to await the arrival of the Leeds train. This 'brief encounter' capped a very enjoyable three days walking in good company and was a very useful preparation for the Pennine Way, which I would commence in just 10 days time.

Three days later I pitched my newly acquired lightweight tent in the front garden and slept in it. I didn't sleep too well as the presence of bright street lights and urban noise made it difficult to do so. I also needed to re-enter the house during the night to use the toilet. I had set myself this 'task' as part of my preparation because I wanted to ensure that I was comfortable with erecting and putting away the tent, just as much as sleeping within it.

CHAPTER TWO

TRAVEL TO EDALE (Wednesday 11th July)

Prior to setting out on my journey I had planned most of the itinerary. Earlier in the year I had planned to spend half the nights under canvas and half the nights in B&B's, but as the summer progressed and the rains continued with both April and June being the wettest of such months since records began, I had revised the itinerary to the extent that now only four nights were planned to be under canvas. This did however mean that as well as the rucksack having clothing and snacks to keep me going for 14 days, I was carrying a tent, sleeping bag and sleeping mat. I decided against taking a camping stove and equipment to cook on. I had also shared my plans with family and friends, so that anyone wanting to accompany me on a part of my journey could do so. I knew before I set off that I would have company on days four and five of the walk and that another friend was joining me for the final three days.

Finally the eve of my departure arrived. I checked the weather forecast and not surprisingly I could expect rain during the first week of my walk; I would need therefore to ensure the clothes I was taking would remain dry. As a consequence I used a number of different bin bags to wrap collections of clothing in before putting them inside the rucksack.

In terms of clothing, I had decided to take two pairs of walking trousers, one that I could unzip the bottoms from and two pairs of walking shorts, four base layers, three mid layers, a lightweight fleece, my cagoule, two pairs of waterproof over-trousers and my sandals to change into. I also had five pairs of high-tec walking socks, four pairs of underpants, a micro towel and a small zip up bag containing my toiletries. I wrapped up in separate bin bags the tent, the sleeping bag and the sleeping mat and secured these with rubber bands.

I had also worked out the most efficient way of securing these to the outside of the rucksack, using the straps and fastenings on the outside of it. I strategically found a place at the bottom front of the bag for the mat, the top front for the tent, which when the top cover was closed, also helped me to secure the sleeping bag in place too.

In addition my pack contained the following food supplies; twelve small packs of dried apricots, fifteen packets of yoghurt coated raisons, four apple bars, six small chocolate bars, two packets of bite size pepperoni snacks, two Kendal mint cake slabs and four other energy bars. I also had a flask for tea/coffee, my water flask and four small cartons of juice. I had a small first aid kit, a small inflatable pillow, my swiss army knife, my mobile phone and charger, 8 OS Maps; that would cover the whole of my route; as well as a guide book, small note book, two pens and a copy of my planned itinerary, including details of the places I was to stay at. Packing and repacking took most of the evening before and the morning of my travelling day. With increasing trepidation however I finally felt satisfied with where everything was and of the weight distribution and comfort of the sack.

Whilst walking the Pennine Way had been a long held ambition and the planning of it this summer had occurred over a number of months, I had also agreed to use the opportunity to fundraise for an all inclusive choir/singing group and had e-mailed a host of people before setting off to make them aware of this. (*ALL ALOUD is an informal singing group, run by volunteer leaders from Bradford Voices. Those attending the weekly sessions don't have to be able to read music, or even be able to read, to join in. The sessions are held in a fully accessible venue and are designed to ensure that all who come can get something out of their attendance. Singing is a proven way to improve feelings of well being, but for many disabled people the opportunity to join a singing group had previously not been available to them).*

About an hour before my departure, Graham, a friend and former work colleague arrived to give me some sponsor money and an article about an account of another Pennine Way journey *(WALKING HOME: Travels with a Troubadour on the Pennine Way by Simon Armitage)* that he had seen reviewed in the Sunday Times. Graham's partners' mother was a resident in a care home near to where I lived and he had taken the opportunity whilst visiting her to drop by to wish me well for the journey. After Graham retired he had undertaken an MA in Railway Studies; one of his passions. He had an encyclopaedic knowledge about both bus and train timetables and it came as no surprise to me that in the envelope he left with me, as well as the article, was an accommodation and transport guide to the Pennine Way.

Sandra gave me a lift to Shipley station to catch the first of the three trains that would convey me to Edale. Whilst en route I had a phone call from John, one of my challenge committee 'comrades' to wish me well. John is a close friend and would have loved to share part of my journey; we had shared many walks in the past; but circumstances meant that he was either working or away on holiday for the duration of this 'expedition'. The train to Leeds was on time and my 'journey' was under way.

I can feel the butterflies tingling now as I finally embark upon, what for me will become, my Pennine Way odyssey. Little do I know of all the adventures I will experience, what the weather holds in store, who I may meet along the way and whether indeed I will be able to complete the trip!

At Leeds I changed platforms to get the Plymouth train, which would take me as far as Sheffield. I found the reserved seat in a packed carriage and spotted someone I knew and had worked with many years before. Sughra had been appointed as an executive officer by my then boss to co-ordinate and support both herself, her Senior Management Team; of whom I was one; and our secretaries. She had left about ten years ago and gone initially to work for, what is now the Care Quality Commission.

The seat across the aisle from me was free so Sughra came to sit there and told me what she was up to and I told her all about my plans for the next two weeks. Whilst in conversation my phone rang again and another friend and former work colleague, Jim was ringing to wish me well. I had originally hoped to stay with Jim and his partner Hazel, at the end of day 3, as he lived in Mytholmroyd, near Hebden Bridge, but unfortunately Jim and Hazel where away at a wedding down South at the weekend. Jim, Graham and John had all been members of my management team within Bradford Council's Adult Services Department.

I said farewell to Sughra as I left the train at Sheffield and made my way to the platform from which my Edale train would depart. The sun was beating down and it was very warm waiting during the twenty minutes or so before an old diesel multiple unit of two carriages trundled in to the station. Apart from two long tunnel stretches there followed a lovely run through the sunny countryside to Edale. Alighting from the train I made my way along the platform, down a ramp and under the track to once more emerge into the sunshine.

I was aware that the 'official' start of the Pennine Way was supposed to be from a pub in Edale and in my eagerness to 'comply with officialdom' I immediately called for a very smooth pint of Grays Bitter at the Rambler Inn; only to learn that the pub I was looking for was a little further on. Oh well I'd just have to have another pint at the Old Nags Head.

This turned out to be another Grays Bitter, although not quite as satisfying as the first one. Despite this I had another pint and felt very contented. Well what better way than to start my journey than by sampling the delights of a pint or three!

I collected my Pennine Way Certificate from the barmaid and in conversation she told me that so far this year only 5 Pennine Way walkers had taken a certificate, or in the case of two local walkers, who were walking North to South, had their certificate verified. Perhaps the wet weather this year had put people off!

I enjoy the short walk to Upper Booth Farm, where I am camping overnight. The campsite was well used with about 20-30 tents of all shapes and sizes virtually filling the first field with maybe 40-50 people; most of whom were teenagers. The farmer had advised me to use the top field anyway and away to the right there are another 8 or 9 tents. At the entrance to the field and just passed a new looking toilet and shower block a group of teenagers were playing football. I found a spot about 5 metres further on from the group of tents and it took me about half an hour to pitch the tent and get everything tidied away. It was about 8pm before I sat down to write a few notes about my day, a pleasant chore which I would repeat at the end of everyday for the next two weeks.

The sun is still shining but there is a breeze. I have no mobile signal to ring or text home to say I am ok, so decide to settle in for the night at 9pm; on reflection probably too early as it is a long while before I get to sleep. In my tent I am excited and a little apprehensive at the prospect of the journey ahead and am itching to get started. I do sleep from about 11pm to 3.30am and then doze on and off till around 5.45. I decide to raid my 'food store' for breakfast at around 6. Up and about I discover that there are about 50 tents in the two fields mainly 1 or 2 berth ones, so there are probably about 75 campers in total on the site. My morning ablutions are completed by 6.30am and I start to pack away the tent, sleeping bag and mat.

CHAPTER THREE

DAY ONE OF THE WALK (EDALE TO CROWDEN)
Thursday 12th July

I was booked in at The Old House B&B at Crowden tonight and by evening would have covered the first 17miles of the PW. At the end of each day I provided a text message of my day's adventures to those who were following my journey and from now on will include at the beginning of each chapter the words I used in my daily messages.

"A good start, set off early and got to my B&B by 3.30pm. Fine weather, although at times very squelchy underfoot. The B&B offer to run you down to a pub about 2.5miles away, where a very reasonably priced early bird meal is available. They will come and pick me up when I have finished. Not bad eh!"

The first morning had dawned with mist on the summits, but it is already starting to burn back in places as I set off at 7.20am. Here's hoping for a rain free day! I leave the campsite and turn right along a narrow road to Lee farm. From here, apart from one or two walkers and navigating my way across the A57 Snake Pass, it is a full day away from civilization. After about half an hour I have a steep climb up Jacob's Ladder; which for some people is the route up to their' view of heaven, taking the walker from Edale to the Kinder plateau. It certainly is quite a steep pull up a 'staircase' of grit stone flags and takes me on to the boulder strewn slopes of Kinder Scout and eventually to the first of the many summits I will visit over the next fourteen days.

At 633 metres Kinder Low will not be the highest, but it feels good to be among the grit stone outcrops and to have a top to share, a photo opportunity and for the first time since the Rambler Inn (yesterday afternoon) I also have a mobile signal and ring home, which enables me to inform Sandra how much I am enjoying the first morning of my long journey. From Kinder Low there are long distance views towards Wales in the west and across the extensive Kinder plateau to the east.

The weather remains dry all day with some warmer sunny periods in the afternoon. Another photo opportunity at Cluther Rocks; nearby to where a Hampden AE381 from RAF 50 Squadron crashed on the 21st January 1942, killing all four crew members. Indeed the Dark Peak is littered with the sites of aircraft crashes, mainly during the war years of the early nineteen forties. I spot the first people of the day, both fell walkers, across the other ridge as I approach Kinder Downfall, which is not as spectacular as I imagined after the recent heavy rains. I enjoy a pleasant walk along the grit stone edge to the semi circular cluster of rocks that mark out Sandy Heys and then on to Mill Hill.

From here I head across squelchy peat bogs, with for about half an hour first one and then a second snipe for company, giving me their distinctive calls and demonstrating their erratic flight patterns. The peat bogs are now covered with a flagstone path which seems to go on forever. I take a break, remove a layer and unzip the legs from my walking trousers and for the rest of the day's walk I remain in shorts. I can see cars which appear to be zipping across the peat bog ahead and eventually realise that it must be the A57, although it is not until I get really close to it that I can actually see the road itself.

I can see and hear a helicopter over the other side off the hill on Bleaklow Head. Two further walkers pass me heading in the opposite direction and the usual walkers' pleasantries are exchanged. After crossing the A57 I encounter a fell runner with his dog and shortly afterwards 6 Duke of Edinburgh trainees, three girls and three boys, who are running slightly behind their schedule. I remember back to my teens and to summer days spent youth hostelling with Nick; my best friend at that time. Whilst we had mainly walked in the Lake District, I also remember a long weekend in the Peak District, when we walked 17 miles and I thought that was ever such a long way. It seems strange that today I will be covering the same distance and yet it will be one of my shorter days!

The track up to Bleaklow Head is long and meandering and follows a stream most of the way; which is apparently the source of the River Derwent and I am constantly fording and re-fording it to keep on the driest land. At one point I overbalance and have a blackened leg from the knee downwards from the peat bog. Whilst I am frustrated at my own clumsiness I do laugh out loud when I look down and see just how filthy my leg is. I stop to wash it and then finally arrive at the summit of Bleaklow Head. (Ironically like Kinder Low at 633m). As I do I get my first clear sight of the helicopter as it ferries rocks to and from a site somewhere on Harry's Moss.

Bleaklow is a high largely peat covered moor land and in poor conditions is probably the most navigationally challenging part of the Peak district. However today the weather is fine, dry and sunny and I have good long distance views. It also boasts the most easterly point in the British Isles above 2000 feet

For the next half an hour the accompanying sound of helicopter blades is as distinctive as that of the snipes earlier in the day. As I start to descend towards Crowden I meet with a man of about 50 who is resting a while at a stile. He was in the army as a young man and recent changes in his life have given him the opportunity and a yearning to do more walking. He is just starting out on what he hopes will be a new chapter in his life.

On learning of my quest he wants to know what the key ingredients to success are, (A reasonable level of fitness, good preparation, the ability to read a map and use a compass, the right equipment and a good dose of determination) he then asks for a quick explanation of using map and compass, as its 30 years since he had to do either back when he was in the army.

After a lengthy chat I carry on and work my way down a steep and at times rocky path until I pause for a breather at a rocky outcrop, where I can sit and I get out my journal to jot down some notes of the day thus far. My recent companion catches up and we again exchange a few pleasantries before he carries on.

The journal writing gets abandoned because of the presence and attention of a host of midges and I carry on down to my night's accommodation.

Just before I get to the road where I will turn off the PW to seek my B&B, I meet another gentleman; about my own age; coming the other way. He is walking from Stalybridge to Glossop. He did the PW in 1983 in 3 weeks and only had 4 hours rain during that time. I'm not sure I'll get away with that! The B&B is great and I have a cup of tea and a slice of Victoria Sponge cake as I sit in the sun and contemplate the wonderful views. I can get a lift to a nearby pub tonight for an evening meal and will get picked up afterwards for a small fee - £2 – well it is 2.5 miles away!

At the pub, the food was good homely fare; plate meat pie, chips and peas, followed by jam roly poly and custard, washed down with two pints of Theakstons Lighter. I am back at the B&B by 8pm and am immediately approached about whether I want a 'full English' in the morning – ah well! I am planning to 'wild camp' on route tomorrow night, somewhere between the A62 and the M62, however if the weather is bad I am advised by my host that I can always camp at the Carriage House near Standedge, as they have showers and a drying room. I calculate that if I cover about 17 miles tomorrow it will give me about another 15 to walk on Saturday, where I am booked in to a B&B about 2 miles beyond Hebden Bridge.

DISTANCE WALKED: 17 MILES

CHAPTER FOUR

DAY TWO : CROWDEN TO HOME! FRIDAY 13TH JULY – UNLUCKY FOR SOME

"Hi all, Rained from leaving B&B at 8.30am until 4pm so just kept plodding on, arrived at Hebden Bridge at 8.30pm – 32 miles. Heading home for a hot bath and to dry out. Now have a short day tomorrow- 5 miles and then back to original schedule. Peter"

I woke at 5am, after a good sleep, to the sound of rain on the velux window. The shower lasted 45 minutes. The forecast is mixed for today. I had a good breakfast and set off at 8.30am in steady rain in cagoule, over trousers and rain cover on the rucksack with the words of 'mine host' ringing in my ears; "Never mind lad it'll fair up soon". He also provided me with his words of advice about the route I should take for the first part of the day's walk.

I retrace my steps to where I left the PW yesterday and work my way down a track and over the dam of one of many reservoirs (Torside) I will 'navigate' around today. I then negotiate the crossing of the A628; one of many roads I will cross today too, and climb for a while and then drop down towards Crowden. The hamlet itself lies further east and has a camping barn and is often the first stop for PW walkers. Strangely enough it lies within the old historic boundaries of Cheshire. The A628, on which it lies, connects Greater Manchester with South Yorkshire.

However before I reach the village, I bear left across sodden grass to climb steadily up a valley side and my path provides lots of fun as I have numerous little (and some larger) streams to ford. At the first of these I plan the stones I will stand on to reach the other side and the rock in the middle that looks perfectly stable gives way and already I have one very wet foot. I stop a little further on to change one sodden sock for a dry one – looking after my feet has to be my mantra on this journey.

I skirt along the narrow escarpment edge of Laddow Rocks; which is a good place for rock climbing – indeed it is said to be the birth place of the sport in the Peak District; before heading down to Crowden Great Brook, where I cross and re-cross the fast flowing stream more times than I can remember, taking great care not to get another wet foot. The rain continues to fall, sometimes relenting to a light drizzle, sometimes increasing to a heavy shower and my mood is getting lower by the minute. Eventually I come to a flagstone path that although underwater in places represents a much 'dryer' path to follow and as it pulls away from this wet boggy morass I make good progress to the top of Black Hill; passing through a larger pool of water before reaching the trig point that marks the summit and is held aloft by a raised circular patio of flagstones with more flagstones encircling it.

This area is called Soldiers' Lump as the Army Royal Engineers who were tasked with erecting the trig point had to create the patio to ensure it could sit on dry land and not sink back into the oozing bog that surrounds it. Black Hill is the most northerly of the grit stone and peaty summits of the Dark Peak. It is a remote and bleak place to be in bad weather, but for me arriving here has lifted my spirits. It is at 1909 feet the highest point in the historic county of Cheshire, but today sits on the boundary between Kirklees in West Yorkshire and High Peak in Derbyshire. I sit in the lee of the prevailing wind (north easterly!) on my little island and have a drink and a bite to eat. It is 11.30am. Apart from my change of sock this is my first stop of the day. I rest for ten minutes and although my mood lightens, the rain doesn't.

As I get to my feet I am surprised to see a young woman (30's) approaching from the other side of my 'island'. I assume she must be equally surprised to see me when she is less than 5 metres from what turns out to be her favourite local summit. She is from a nearby village – Marsden, and the trig point is the destination for her walk. Her husband did the PW a few years ago and she has two daughters (7&5) and she hopes they will all do the PW together one day. I leave her to the solitude of Black Hill and the one spot there that is sheltered from the wind and rain. As I leave the summit the rain increases in intensity again and continues as such for about 30 minutes as I head down the other side of Black Hill to the A635 road at Wessenden Head.

The young lady has already informed me that the refreshment van that "usually parks there" according to my guide book, no longer does, so my one 'guaranteed' supply of fresh food for the day is scuppered, however my larder supply of snacks is still pretty full. Just before the road, the path dips down sharply to a gully that has two gushing streams to cross with an 'island' of a grassy hump in between. Once across the path zigzags and climbs steeply up to the road. As I reach it I turn to look back and see the woman I spoke to at the summit coming down towards the dip. *(See Chapter Nine for an account of what happened to four PW walkers who arrived at this spot later in the day)*

After crossing the road and bearing left down a minor road for about 200 metres I head down to the Wessenden Head reservoir. A brief 5 minute respite from the rain allows a quick stop for a drink and a sandwich. I then head gently down now alongside a second reservoir before arriving at a confluence of tracks and a cluster of buildings and briefly the PW joins the Kirklees Way. It then drops down steeply back on itself to the left to an outlet stream of the reservoir. The rain is getting heavier again as is my heart and I start to wonder whether I will be able to manage to complete my self imposed Pennine Way challenge. Just then I spot a goldfinch on a thistle – one of the highlights of the day. This small and dainty bird with its red head and bright yellow flashes, clinging on to the swaying thistle, as it is buffeted by the wind and rain, cheers me up no end.

About 100 metres down the slope a rocky outcrop with an overhang allows another stop and a perfect place to change over map pages. A mother with a daughter (in her early teens) and a dog pass me at this point, but are soon re-passed, as the mother beckons me to go ahead as we approach a steep climb out of the valley to a stone monument. There follow long and twisty energy sapping stretches now which, apart from one short steep pull, rise up gently until two more reservoirs appear (Black Moss and Swellens). The path takes me between them and along the side of the second before veering right, where I can see the A62 road and Standedge beyond.

Ahead lies another reservoir with what I at first think are tents pitched by it. These later are obviously identified as upturned boats. Redbrook reservoir, obviously in much fairer weather than today, might tempt one to go sailing on it. It apparently has a small and friendly club that offers unrestricted sailing and facilities for compatible pursuits. I decide to 'sail on' myself, as my plan for the day was always to get beyond Standedge to look for somewhere suitable to pitch the tent for the night.

However suddenly a Plan B for the day emerges in my head – just keep walking to Hebden Bridge and get the train back home for the night. The following day I can get the train back and rejoin the PW. For the rest of the day, and over the next hour in particular, this plan gets analysed and re-analysed as I toy with the logistics, practicalities, distances, and time and transport possibilities. Would there be a risk I might just decide to stay at home and abandon the walk if I went with this plan? It would also mean walking two miles off route at the end of the day and another two miles to rejoin it tomorrow, thereby adding four extra miles to my journey.

After I cross the A62 I climb steadily and suddenly realise that I haven't had a break or a drink for a while and am starting to feel tired and a little dehydrated. As there is a broken stone wall to my left I work my way round to the other side to seek some protection from the wind and rain. I also find I have a mobile signal and ring home. It is 3.30pm, I explain to Sandra that I am still walking and am somewhere between the A62 and the

M62 and that apart from a 5 minute respite it has rained for all of the duration of the day's walk so far.

I do not discuss Plan B, as at this stage I don't want to put pressure on myself by committing to it. I carry on in the rain and start to dream of the possibility of a refreshment van on the A627 Saddleworth Moor Road (I have seen them parked there before) just before the M62 – no such luck!

As I reach the Trig point on the grassy summit of White Hill, I spot the rather large Telecommunications mast that I have seen many times when crossing the M62 east to west. I spend about 20 minutes, which seems more like thirty, walking towards it, when suddenly at 4pm I become aware that the rain as stopped. It is still grey and dreary as my first sight of the M62 comes into view. I can see that traffic is stationery going east. I am suddenly glad to be out walking and not stuck down there in a traffic jam. I stop to find my camera to take my first picture of the day – a motorway! I have a quick drink and my last sandwich on the footbridge that 'hangs' high above the motorway and briefly reflect on the fact that the rain has meant many missed photo opportunities earlier in the day.

It seems to take a good while for the sound of the motorway to die away as I start my steady climb up Blackstone Edge. Whilst it is not raining I am walking in low cloud and mist with the wind still blowing hard. A rock on the left looms out of the mist appearing like a huge head in silhouette.

A shelter just before the summit is built in the shape of a 'C' with protection on the inside from 3 sides – as the usual prevailing weather normally comes from the south west. As I have been buffeted all day by north easterlies it offers me no protection whatsoever and I carry on to the summit trig point and across a boulder strewn landscape made even more eerie by the swirling mists.

Finding the path amongst the boulders is tricky for a while but eventually it becomes easier as I start to descend. At the Aiggin Stone – a medieval landmark – I turn left down hill and can see Littleborough far below. I then follow a much leveller and easier path for a while along the broad head drain before dropping down steeply to another road; the A58. I can see the White House pub to my right and suddenly a Plan C emerges. If the White House do accommodation and have a vacancy I could stay there for the night. Even if they don't, a 20 minute break to get out of the wind and have a pint and contemplate the rest of the day seems a very valid option.

As I reach the road I can see at least three cars parked in the car park, but as I get closer I can tell it is not open. Tables are laid inside, but there is absolutely no sign of life. I carry on with Plan C in tatters and in a foul mood and take the next turn to walk along a path across the dam of the Blackstone edge reservoir. The path then bends round past the head drain where an 'Ode to Rain' is beautifully inscribed on the rock-face and my mood is immediately lifted, both at the words themselves and at the beauty of the carving and at finding such beauty in such an unlikely place.

I am reminded of the article that Graham left with me just before I set off. I am sure that this writing is the work of Simon Armitage; local poet, who last year walked the Pennine Way North to South, giving poetry readings each evening to earn enough to pay for his accommodation and food during his journey. I make a mental note to myself to check this out when I return. *(See the note at the end of this Chapter for further information)* The path then takes me on to two more reservoirs, which stretch in an arc as far as the eye can see.

The wind is relentless here and coming from my right with absolutely no shelter or protection whatsoever and to cap it all the rain returns after a two hour respite. After about a mile and half way along the second reservoir (Warland), the open rails to my right give way to a solid stone wall, about four feet high which provides a temporary relief behind which to shelter from the wind and rain. I have a hot drink and a bar of chocolate. By now it is 6pm and my calculations on arrival time at Hebden Bridge have now been refined to the point where I think I will be there at 9pm at the latest – time enough to get a train to Bradford and be home by 11pm. Plan B is now definitely the option I am going for.

After the Warland Reservoir the path bears a 90 degree turn to the right and I can see Stoodley Pike clearly, maybe 2/3 miles away. I carry on and pass the start of the path which drops down into Mankinholes, where two of my fellow overnighters at The Old Barn where headed for: 27 miles we had calculated last night would be the distance to walk for them. I start to play mind games with myself as I calculate my ETA at Stoodley Pike. I'm two minutes out and am there by 7pm.

The Pike itself is a 121 foot monument, which dominates the moor land horizon for miles around. It was designed by a local architect James Green in 1854 and completed in 1856 at the end of the Crimean War. It is thought to have replaced an earlier structure built to commemorate the defeat of Napolean at the Battle of Waterloo. There have been times today when I thought I was going to meet my Waterloo!

I ring home to finally confirm my plan B for the evening /night and get the answer phone, so leave a message for Sandra to ring me. Descending Stoodley Pike I have my first navigational error of the day. I see a signpost which says 2 miles to Callis Bridge and another half a mile further on another which says two and three quarter miles to Callis Bridge. On re-consulting the map/guide book I decide that I should have gone straight down at a grass bank to a stile and retrace my steps for 200 metres. Oh joy! The short grass bank leads to a stile into a field containing about twenty or so bullocks; who now block my way and a few anxious moments are taken up with 'shooing' and edging forward until I can continue to another stile.

I am now walking through a field of long wet grass. After 29 miles of protecting my boots from getting over wet; apart from the earlier foot in the water mishap; I can feel them soaking up the water and my feet getting pretty wet too. I inwardly curse the fool that felt that running the footpath through a field of long grass (particularly at the end of a long weary day) would be a good idea.

Whilst crossing this field my mobile rings and it is Sandra responding to my message. I explain my Plan B and as luck would have it she is in Bradford shopping, so will stay around and pick me up from Bradford station. I agree to ring her once I am on the train and know what time it will arrive at Bradford.

I go through a farm and down a track with a steep bank up to a stone wall to my left and a steep drop down to a stream to my right and find myself faced with a group of cows and young calves. As I walk down this winding track and pass most of the herd, I see two young calves are ahead. The further I descend the more they stay in front of me. Suddenly I am aware of a bellowing behind me as mother has come to be reunited with her young. I leave the relative safety of the track to scramble up and along the steep bank to my left until I am in front of the calves and can descend again to the track. Throughout this manoeuvre the 'mooing' of the mother is getting louder and louder. Thankfully the calves and mother are now reunited and I can continue downwards to Callis Bridge. As I do so I meet a cyclist coming up the track and I caution him to be aware of loopy calves and an overprotective mother.

Finally I reach the road at Callis Bridge and then leave the PW for the day as I walk the two miles along the A646 to Hebden Bridge. I arrive at the station at about 8.40pm. There is a train at 9.05 which gets to Bradford at 9.35pm, so I ring Sandra to tell her this. There is a cafe / bar at the station and I have a well earned half of locally brewed Cragg Vale organic bitter and a packet of crisps whilst waiting for the train. Once on it, I am joined by around 14 – 16 teenagers, who are off to sample the evening delights of Halifax and I find the excited hubbub of conversation quite a sharp contrast to what has gone before.

I am pleased to see Sandra at the station and offload the rucksack into the boot. Once at home a hot bath is the number one priority, this is followed by stuffing boots with paper and laying out clothes to dry. A bite to eat and a night's sleep in my own bed complete what has been a rather extraordinary, long and weary day.

At times I have felt very low, the walking I have enjoyed, but the combination of the weather and the underfoot conditions made me doubt my sanity at taking on this challenge.

DISTANCE WALKED TODAY: 32 MILES

TOTAL DISTANCE WALKED: 49 MILES

FOOTNOTE:

The Ode to Rain was indeed written by Simon Armitage and was part of the Stanza Stones Project. In 2010 Ilkley Literature Festival and imove, commissioned Simon to create a series of poems responding to the landscape of the Pennine Watershed in the run up to London 2012. The Festival asked letter carver Pip Hall to carve Simon's poems in six atmospheric locations along the watershed from Marsden, where Simon was born to Ilkley – the home of the Festival.

CHAPTER FIVE

HOME TO BLACKSHAW HEAD (Saturday 14th July)

"Hi all, short day/walk today – 4 miles. Got my boots and clothes dry. Now back on schedule and looking forward to tomorrow when I will have a walking companion for part of the day. Peter"

It feels very strange to be waking up in my own bed. Although it is only three mornings ago that I was doing this, it seems a long time ago. I am suddenly aware of how much I have packed in to my journey so far. Far from wanting to 'give up' on my quest I feel strangely re-energised and even more determined to get back to the PW and carry on with my journey.

The only problem with coming home is getting wrapped up in domesticity again. I don't need to catch a train back to Hebden Bridge until this afternoon, as I only have the two miles from the station to rejoin the PW and then a further 2 miles to get to the B&B I had previously booked for Saturday night. Sandra is also going to be away for a few days and has arranged for one of our dogs to be looked after by her brother and sister-in-law in Farnworth. The irony of this is that about 11am in the morning I am driving east to west along the M62, spotting the telecommunications tower I was heading towards from the south yesterday and then at the high point of the route travelling under and pointing out to Sandra, the footbridge that I walked across less than 24 hours earlier.

Back at home I repacked the rucksack and left behind two pairs of wet and dirty walking socks, a pair of underpants and a base layer. I replaced both the underpants and base layer on a like for like basis. However I had no more high tech walking socks at home so picked out a pair of walking socks I had used for shorter walking trips in the past and put these in an outside pocket of the rucksack, intending to use them as an emergency pair only. I also asked Sandra if once the two high tech pairs were washed and dried she could take them with her on her trip up to visit our grand daughter in Whitley Bay next week. She would no doubt be meeting with Christine (Trevor's wife) and could ensure he had them to pass back to me so I would have them for the last three days walking.

It almost felt like starting again as later in the afternoon I got a lift down to the station in time to catch the 3.30pm train to Hebden Bridge. From the station I retrace my steps of yesterday evening as I walk the two miles along the main road back to Callis Bridge to rejoin the PW. It feels strange to be doing this and walking along a main road is not at all what this journey is about. Thankfully it is Sunday and the traffic is fairly light. I feel a real surge of adrenalin when I am finally reunited with the PW, which is just as well as I then have a very steep pull up to the B&B, past clusters of houses clinging perilously it seems to the hillside at times. My abode for the evening/night is very comfortable and Miriam, my hostess, very welcoming and I am soon sitting in the garden enjoying a cup of tea and a slice of cake, surveying the wonderful scenery and looking back across the valley to Stoodley Pike where I was some 22 hours earlier.

The B&B offered a cooked evening meal and when I booked it the plan was to rough camp last night and feast on a cold supper from my provisions store, and then to walk about 16 miles, so the prospect of a cooked evening meal seemed very appealing at that time. I felt therefore a little bit of a fraud sitting down to a meal after only an hour and a half's walk. However the meal was in actual fact very good, pork loin with mustard mash, creamed carrots and home grown spring cabbage, followed by Bakewell tart and custard.

I retire early to sort out my rucksack and rearrange clothes and to write up two days of the diary of my PW journey and send off my daily texts to those following my progress.

DISTANCE WALKED TODAY: 4 MILES

TOTAL DISTANCE WALKED: 53 MILES

CHAPTER SIX

BLACKSHAW HEAD TO COWLING (Sunday 15th July)

"Hi all, 15 miles today in good weather and good company for 2nd half of the day (Mo) Martin walking with me tomorrow. Am feeling good – only 210 miles to go. Peter"

I wake at 6am, after a good sleep, with the sun streaming through the window. After sorting out my rucksack (again) I shower and get dressed, short sleeves and shorts, and go downstairs for breakfast. I decide on scrambled eggs on toast rather than a full English breakfast and say my farewells to Gordon and Miriam. I leave the farmhouse and its beautiful gardens at 8.30 am hoping to rendezvous with Maureen at between 12 and 12.15 at Ponden Reservoir.

The first hour is a bit fiddly, negotiating fields and stiles and gates, until I am once more amongst more open moor land. Whilst crossing Heptonstall Moor I find a large brightly coloured pheasant feather and pick it up and store it between the plastic folds at the top of my map case. I intend to give it to Maureen to take back to Sandra as a memento of my journey. My route drops down to yet another reservoir – Gorple Lower, with good views across to the Pack Horse away to my right.

After crossing the path at the head of the reservoir I head down to a minor road in the distance and am passed in both directions by pairs of cyclists enjoying the Sunday morning sunshine.

I reach the road at Clough Foot and cross a short bank to join another tarmac road that rises steeply besides a wood to my left. This provides protection from the stiff breeze, for a while, as I start to catch one of the pairs of cyclists. However the road levels out again and then drops down to Walshaw Dean and they are soon way ahead. I leave the road and bear down to Walshaw Dean Reservoir and take another picture across water.

As I head on I recognize my surroundings and realise that I have walked the next couple of miles of the PW before as part of a walk from Hardcastle Crags. Whilst I am racking my brains to remember when it was I suddenly realise that I have lost my beautiful feather. After a quick debate with myself I decide not to waste time on a probably fruitless search and carry on. I decide that this stretch is probably one that Sandra could walk with me in the future. Sandra is not a great walker of hills, but does enjoy shorter walks in the countryside. The underfoot conditions are not too bad and I surmise during a 'normal summer' would be very good and the scenery across the reservoir gives plenty of interest too. Wrapped in such thoughts I almost tread on a small ugly toad that is squatting on the path.

A further reservoir offers another photo shoot and a pleasant walk beside it before I strike up towards Top Withins.

Top Withins is a ruined farmhouse on the moors above Howarth and is widely considered to be the inspiration for the Earnshaw family house, 'Wuthering Heights' in the novel of the same name written by Emily Bronte. I have walked to here before with Sandra and my daughters' Becky and Jenny, when they were both teenagers. We had parked near the bus terminus at Stanbury and followed the paths and tracks up to this desolate, yet evocatively beautiful spot.

I had calculated I would be there by 11.30am and my progress across the moors from the reservoir is such that I do actually arrive at Top Withins at exactly that time. I pause to text Maureen to tell her where I am and that I should be at Ponden in 30 minutes as planned. A pleasant, if winding descent follows and once at Ponden Reservoir I ring Maureen to check on her whereabouts. Her public transport arrangements haven't quite worked out as planned and she is walking further as a consequence from Howarth and this means our link up time will be around 12.30. I take the opportunity to have a break for a drink and some crisps. As Maureen comes into view along the path I had followed too, it's good to see a friendly and familiar face. I greet Maureen and we walk on together for about 10 minutes before we find a wall that provides some shelter from the wind sufficient for us to have lunch.

I have known Maureen and her partner Tel for over twenty years. Maureen and Tel have three children of similar ages to my daughters. Maureen has always had a love of the great outdoors and she has walked with me and other friends too on a number of occasions. One of Maureen's great outdoor adventures was to walk the Via de La Plata in Spain and I had agreed to share the first week of that walk with her. We found then that we tended to walk at a similar pace and I was pleased to have her as a walking companion on part of my journey today.

After our lunch stop there were some more fiddly bits before we emerged onto Oakworth Moor and find a path that leads to the summit of Bare Hill, where a path leads down and to the right to Keighley Moor Reservoir. Our path goes straight on and then appears to head directly to the summit and rocks of Great Wolf Stones. However before it reaches them it veers right before heading over heathery moor land and we arrive at a shelter at Cat Stone Hill. Here we spend a pleasant 20 minutes or so having a drink, a snack and a chat about life, families and walking. I had really enjoyed sharing the first week of Maureen's longest walk. The 'Via de la Plata', or Pilgrim Way in Spain runs from Seville in the South to Santiago in the North. Maureen had taken around six weeks to cover the 600 or so miles.

I had walked with her for the first 96 miles from Seville to Zafra.

Heading down off the moor now, with Cowling Pinnacle and Lund's Tower to our right, we arrive at a pleasant waterfall at Lumb. *Lund's Tower was apparently built by James Lund of Malsis Hall reputedly for his daughter Ethel. A narrow spiral staircase twists round and up the inside to give wonderful 360 degree panoramic views from the top.* The waterfall is set against a very green backcloth and presents an ideal image for a photograph.

From here the path bends round and then drops through fields to the A6068 below. My B&B for the night is only a 100metres down from where the PW crosses the main road and I know that Maureen can get a bus back to Keighley from here and from there a bus back home.

We head for the B&B with the intention of testing the possibility of Maureen joining me for a cup of tea before she departs and have trouble gaining entry. That is until we discover the proprietor and a friend in a shed to the right of the main house. The shed is full of model helicopters of varying sizes and in various stages of construction. We are regaled for a little while in stories about helicopters before Maureen is able to join me for a cup of tea and is able to use the facilities before walking a further 100 metres down the road to the bus stop.

I shower and change and then walk into Cowling for a pint at the pub (Wainwrights). They don't do food, but not far away and nearer to the B&B there is an Indian restaurant at which I can dine and I am back at the B&B soon after 8pm. Having sent my daily text I check that Martin is still on to join me tomorrow; he is. Apparently the B&B had a phone call from someone asking to speak to me whilst I was out and I surmise this might have been from my brother in France; as he has my itinery and has said he would ring me at some stage during my journey.

As I sit down to write the notes from the day's walk it starts to rain – hopefully not a sign of things to come tomorrow. So far I have walked to and/or alongside 14 reservoirs and climbed 7 peaks over 1500 feet. As I am musing on this my phone rings and it is my brother in France ringing back to check on my progress and have a quick update.

DISTANCE WALKED TODAY: 14 MILES

TOTAL DISTANCE WALKED: 67 MILES

CHAPTER SEVEN

COWLING TO ABOVE MALHAM TARN (Monday 16th July)

" Hi all, 19 miles completed to Malham with Martin. Mostly in rain with muddy fields and numerous stiles. Having a 2 hour break for a hot meal and a couple of pints of Copper dragon! 3 more miles this evening before I pitch for the night. It has stopped raining. Peter"

I again wake to the sound of rain, but by the time I am showered, dressed and ready for breakfast, it seems to have stopped. A very pleasant full English breakfast and whilst Gordon has his helicopter stories, Miriam, his wife, is able to regale one with stories about the property, having lived in it all her life, apart from a break of 7 years when she and Gordon were first married. Her grandmother lived there too.

Martin arrives about 8.50am and we set off walking at 9am as planned. He is able to leave his car at the B&B and will pick it up later in the day, (as it turns out a lot wetter and a lot wiser). For the first thirty minutes of our walk we are without rain, but from then on I am in waterproofs and over-trousers until about 2pm in Gargrave. Unfortunately Martin has left his over-trousers in his car, but thankfully not his cagoule as well. The morning's route takes one through a maze of often sodden fields and over lots of fiddly stiles. In one of the first fields we spot a hare as it races away into longer grass and is lost from view. It isn't long before my boots are sodden again.

I have known Martin for about 3 years, initially as an HR consultant to another Voluntary Organisation and for the last two years also as an HR consultant to Disability Advice Bradford. However we had never had the opportunity to spend time together in a non-work context and it was surprising how much we have in common and how much we found to chat about as we followed the PW on its meandering course to Gargrave and then on to Malham.

The conversation covers running, books on the fells, families and lots of other stuff too. After negotiating many fields and stiles we emerge onto the southernmost side of the Leeds to Liverpool Canal and head eastwards under bridge number 160, where we spot a family of ducks and it provides Martin with an opportunity to take a picture. We carry on towards, then under, a rather curious double arched bridge (161). This carries the busy A59 road from Skipton through to the Lakes and is a road I have often travelled. We leave the canal just before bridge 162 and head towards Gargrave.

The Dalesman cafe' at Gargrave is not open on Mondays' and neither it seems are any other cafes. This turns out to be more of a heartbreaking moment for Martin, as he discovers that he has also left the sandwiches he lovingly prepared this morning back in the car too. So we carry on after a brief stop to raid our provisions supplies. Luckily Martin has not left everything edible behind, otherwise he would have had to sample dried apricots or yoghurt coated raisons or bite sized pepperoni or even a healthy energy bar! I suppose I have got into the habit of snacking during my walking days, rather than having a single and longer lunch stop.

As the conversation turns to the broad subject of education we get so engrossed that we miss the turn off where the PW leaves a minor road, to once more cross wet and often muddy fields. The track is pretty vague at times and before long we have to consult map and guide book to work out where we are and indeed have to retrace steps again to find our correct route. This becomes a bit of a pattern to our day as the more engrossed in conversation we get, the greater the risk of losing the PW. We come to a maze of gates that have within them a churned up morass of mud and debate negotiating them to access a field on the furthest side. We both agree that this is not a good plan and retrace our steps again. During this time we have to negotiate fields with cows and bulls in them; within which Martin is happy for me to take the lead, due to my growing experience of sensing whether any may propose a risk to us or not. In addition there are the endless stiles and the clinging mud. These factors all add up to an extra mile or so by the time we get to Malham.

We even have an encounter with a cow that moments before has just given birth. It is clear that the afterbirth is still to appear and she is very protective of her new born calf. The challenge for us is that she has decided to give birth in the corner of a field, right in front of the stile we should be taking to access the road we need to cross. We are headed to the corner to cross a stile to our left and then should be taking a stile in a wall at right angles to the one in the first stile. We carefully cross the stile and then skirt well away from and round the cow and calf and head for a gate in the second wall about thirty metres away. Luckily we are able to open it and escape the field on to the road. We retrace our steps to pick up the path on the other side of the road opposite the stile we should have crossed. The cow was certainly in no mood to let anyone near her calf.

Whilst I remember well hearing snipe, curlews and oystercatchers the abiding memories of this stretch were of wet grass and mud and endless stiles. The route along the river Aire to Malham is particularly sodden and it is with great relief that we arrive there at 5.15pm and as the rain has returned seek refuge in the Buck Inn.

We enjoy two pints of delicious and refreshing Copper Dragon and Martin rings for a taxi to take him back to Cowling to be reunited with his car and more importantly his lunch! I don't think he can quite believe that after a fairly hard day's walking, mostly in the rain, I am now preparing to carry on and plan to bed down under canvas out in the wilds and not find a local B&B; that may offer a warm bath and a comfortable bed for the night.

However after he is gone, I order a lasagne; finish the second pint and then jot down my notes of the day's walk. My intention is to walk for a further 3 miles or so this evening and to find a suitable spot to pitch the tent for the night. After a break of two hours therefore I leave the comfort of the Buck Inn and head off towards Malham Cove to negotiate the numerous steps that help me quickly to gain altitude but present quite a challenge at the end of the day. Not slipping on the limestone escarpment at the top of the cove presents a further challenge as I head on towards Malham tarn, as do several adjustments to my rucksack as it seems not to be clinging to me as snugly as before. It becomes a bit of a slog to get to and then past the tarn and I debate whether to pitch the tent at the tarn itself, but decide that it may be too open and breezy there. Finally at about 8.45pm I find the area I believed from consulting the map would provide the best camping option and I spend 5 minutes clearing slugs from it before pitching the tent.

Once inside I take off wet boots and socks and dry my feet and put on the dry pair of socks I packed when I was at home last Saturday morning; this later turns out to be a mistake! I am dry and warm inside the tent. I reflect on the day and recall the highlights; the hare dashing through the field early in the day, the countryside around the river Aire in the afternoon; when the rain finally stopped for a while and of course, Martin's company. It rains intermittently through the night and whilst I do get some sleep at about 5.30am I decide to start to get ready to leave and eat some yoghurt coated raisins and a chocolate bar for breakfast; it makes a change from dried apricots. I start trying to pack things away and keep them as dry as possible, rather a challenge as the day has dawned damp and misty. I end up keeping on the socks I changed into the evening before, rather than extricating a higher 'spec' pair from the depths of the rucksack.

DISTANCE WALKED TODAY: 22 MILES

TOTAL DISTANCE WALKED: 89 MILES

CHAPTER EIGHT

ABOVE MALHAM TARN TO HAWES (Tuesday 17th July)

"Hi all, now in Hawes. Today hardest day so far. Set off from where I camped overnight in rain and mist at 6.30am; climbed Fountains Fell and Pen-y-gent by 10am. Then dropped down to Horton-in-Ribblesdale for lunch. It then stopped raining for a short while until 2pm. Then 15 mile walk to Hawes – 27 miles in total, had the first kit malfunction and first blisters. It's currently hammering it down. Shorter day tomorrow – 17 miles and I get to the half way mark. A good sleep will sort me out. Peter"

I discover that the problem I was having with the rucksack yesterday, in particular with the waist straps, was because one side was torn away and is hanging by only one set of stitching. I had chosen the sack based on its capacity, the convenience and variety of pockets that matched my requirements and the comfort and adjustability of the shoulders, back and waist banding. Although it normally retailed at £90, I bought it in the sale at half that price and as such it was relatively inexpensive for a rucksack of such a high specification.

For the rest of my journey I am especially careful when loading or offloading it to ensure I do not put any undue pressure on the spot. By the end of today what is also becoming an irritant is continually (six or seven times during the day) having to relocate the top strap, where it clips on to a seam.

Maybe on reflection the lack of a good nights' sleep, a long day in mostly poor weather and the fact my socks start to rub and later in the day I get blisters may have some influence on my propensity to become irritated! My irritation is as much inwardly directed at my own failure to properly look after my feet today; which has been my own self confessed mantra for this walk and the fact that this may now put pay to my ability to complete it.

The first four hours of the morning are spent in mist and the kind of light rain that 'wets you right through'. My 6.30am start takes me on a route that involves climbing Fountains' Fell; too wet and misty for a photo; and then onto and up the steep slopes of Pen-y-gent. At one point between the two I suddenly discover I have a mobile signal and ring home to confirm I have survived the night and am under way again. When I finally arrive at the summit of Pen-y-gent it is about 10am. I sit in the shelter there for fifteen minutes, having a bite to eat and a drink and contemplating whether I am enjoying my 'holiday' and ruminating on the meaning of life! For me we are all only here once and I believe need to ensure that what we make of our lives we can look back on in later life with some degree of pride and at the same time not have a dossier of regrets to ponder on. The PW for me fits entirely into this scenario. I have wanted to do this walk for a very long time. I do want to be able to look back on it and feel some sense of achievement about it. I also know myself well enough to be clear that if, during my life, I had never set out on this journey I would have always regretted not doing so.

I am brought out of my 'blue period' when a single 'three peaker' arrives at the summit and we engage in some banter, he is quickly followed by a pair of three-peakers. This couple had done the PW in 2006 and were really gushing about the Horton to Hawes leg of the walk, which I would be covering during the afternoon. (*Three peakers are hikers who are out to walk the three Yorkshire Peaks of, Whernside, Pen-y-gent and Ingleborough in one day*).

I had climbed Pen-y-gent from Horton-in-Ribblesdale before so was familiar with the descent down into the village and finally the rain stopped and the mist cleared at the lower levels and I began to enjoy life again. The famous Pen-y-gent cafe' was closed; this seems to becoming a familiar theme; so I went to and used the very nice public toilets to deal with a bit of chaffing on the inside of my left thigh that was bothering me. It took me a while to find the antiseptic cream, de-rucksack and disrobe sufficiently to be able to address the reddened area and then get dressed again. In retrospect if only I had taken the opportunity to examine my feet and change my socks too!

I then went to the pub *(Well it was the only other place I would be able to get something to eat!)* for lunch before heading the 15 or so miles on to Hawes. It was 11.40am and the sign on the door of the Crown said; "Open at 11.30-ish" A bloke was sitting outside at a picnic table and confidently asserted that they would be open any minute. I broke from my usual tradition; of not drinking alcohol until the end of the day's walk; and had a half and was about to order a sandwich, when I was advised that 'they don't serve food till 12'. I decide to stay a bit longer and at 12 precisely order a Wensleydale cheese sandwich; which arrives with a substantial salad, coleslaw and a bowl of chips. I end up wrapping one of the sandwiches up in a serviette to eat later.

I leave the Crown and rejoin the PW, which goes back up on to the fells from the car park behind the pub.

One of the things I like about undertaking a long walk is that on each day there is only one objective; getting from point A to point B. It is possible therefore to let go of all the other things that if I had been at home, I could or should have been doing. Getting from A to B not only defines the day, but it frees my mind to dream, to enjoy the landscape and to feel completely grounded within and at one with that landscape; whether it is grit stone outcrops, reservoirs, moor-land tracts, limestone escarpments, boggy lowlands or lofty heights. I am also very self driven once I have set my mind to something, which is why as soon as lunch is over, the 'journey' must continue. I also know I have a good 27 miles to cover and that I am not yet halfway along today's journey of (self) discovery.

The route is up hill; or so it seems; for the next nine miles and is steep at times, with shallower gentle rises at other times. After about a mile I get the chance to look down into a sink hole to my right; Sell Gill Hole; there are certainly plenty of sink holes in the area. As I do so I spot a rather nice feather on the ground and pick it up and store it in the folds of the map case, maybe this one will remain with me for a little longer than the last one! At about 3pm the rain returns and whilst it is not heavy, my cagoule is once more required.

Despite it now being my constant companion for the rest of the day, I continue walking in my shorts.

The route climbs steadily to Birkwith Moor. The nature reserve of Ling Gill, which follows a long narrow valley, through which Cam Beck; a tributary of the River Ribble runs; is interesting. as is the old stone pack horse bridge used to cross Cam Beck. Ling Gill is a rare example of sub-alpine ash woodland and a site of scientific interest and is fenced off to protect it from both unwanted grazing and from the public. This is to protect the fragile fauna and flora it supports. Once past the area of woodland I arrive at the old pack horse bridge, which I suspect has been used to cross Cam Beck here for several centuries. I am sure that the dark peaty swirling water rushing under it will enjoy its journey through Ling Gill.

I then become conjoined to the Cam High Road; a track; which stretches ahead forever and ever. I am sure in fine weather, when you have views to look at it may be a different kettle of fish, but today it's not 'rocking my boat'. I am also conscious of the rough and stony conditions underfoot which are starting to hurt my feet!

I have walked two miles of the Cam Road before as part of the Dales Way with John and Simon, although we were walking down it not up it and in dry and bright conditions. Ironically that was the last time I had had any trouble with blisters on a walk. The rain and mist are now all enveloping and it is just a case of plodding on. The Cam Road eventually becomes a tarmac road at just above 2000 feet before it follows the contours of Dodd Fell Hill on its endless journey to Hawes. As it finally descends, there is a particularly difficult bit where loads of boulders have been dropped on the track and are strewn all around making walking and staying upright quite a challenge. Whilst negotiating these beastly obstacles I miss the PW going off to the right; which would I am sure have provided some relief from my plight; and I am now stuck with the Cam Road almost all the way to Hawes.

I also realise that I am now featherless again; ah well maybe I just wasn't meant to have a 'physical memento' of the walk after all. My feet are really sore, but as I am so close to Hawes, I just want to get there now and get out of the wind and the rain. Finally there is an opportunity to cut across another track to rejoin the PW for the last half a mile to Hawes. It is now raining even more heavily and I arrive, dripping wet, at the B&B (The Black Bull) at 6.30pm.

My feet are sore and a number of angry blisters have appeared and whilst I have been dreaming of a soak in a hot tub for the last few hours, it turns out the en suite in my room is a shower, so getting clean again is more of a challenge, as is sorting out my feet. It takes a while to get clean and dry, dressed and to give my feet the attention they need; thank goodness for my supply of 'Compeed'. I have used Compeed plasters before and they are an essential part of my kit when undertaking a walk of any distance. They act like a second skin to support the natural moisture balance and they do remove blister pain very effectively.

Having completed these tasks I send off my daily texts and then go in search of food and a pint, as the rain hammers down on the windows and roof of the B&B. My spirits are lifted again and despite more rain forecast for tomorrow, I am looking forward to the journey to the Tan Hill. The longer term forecast predicts a dry sunny day for Saturday and for real July weather for the last two days of my walk! We shall see. The first pub I call at has stopped serving food, but there is another next door and I enjoy a very fine fish and chips and, given where I am staying, an appropriately named, and very pleasant, pint of Theakstons Black Bull.

Hawes is a bustling market town in the heart of Wensleydale, with many gift and craft shops and places to stay. The surrounding area has lots of great walks and scenery and therefore it remains ever popular as a place both to visit and stay at. In the fading light and in teeming rain it is not selling itself very well to me, but it is after all just a stopping off point on a longer journey of discovery.

The room at the B&B has a huge bed and in the middle of it is a huge teddy bear. I decide to sleep alone though and prop teddy up on a chair in the corner. I manage to get some clothes washed and dried during the night, but I do now have a growing bag of dirty washing within the rucksack. My boots have been packed with newspapers and are almost dry by morning. I use my swiss army knife to scrape of excess mud and they start to resemble the footwear I set off in again.

DISTANCE WALKED TODAY: 27 MILES

TOTAL DISTANCE WALKED: 116 MILES

CHAPTER NINE

HAWES TO TAN HILL (Wednesday 18th July)

"Hi all, Now at Tan Hill Inn – half way. This morning was hell, but this afternoon pretty good. AM Summary: mist, rain, hail, gale force winds, saturated and boggy ground and 6 miles up hill to summit of Great Shunner Fell. Never has a summit shelter been more welcome. Sunshine, views and a pleasant walk this pm. Peter"

The day starts with the best breakfast of the trip so far and I have slept well in my extra large bed. Having togged up in my waterproofs I settle the bill and head off in the rain on a short stretch of about a mile to Hardraw. I don't deviate from the PW to visit Hardraw Force however, as I have seen this, the largest single drop waterfall in England, before.

The rain stops; which was forecast; however the respite lasts for only fifteen minutes (*this wasn't forecast*) and having left the B&B at 8.50am it takes me until 12.15pm to negotiate the long, arduous, wet, boggy climb to Great Shunner Fell summit. Not only do I have awful underfoot conditions to contend with, but the wind is the fiercest it has been all week and at times the driving rain has hail mixed in with it. If you add to this the swirling mist and the fact that I am struggling to see through my glasses; it becomes a heady cocktail of challenges. If I thought yesterday was hard, the first four hours of today completely surpass that.

Finally the cross shelter and summit cairn loom out of the mist and I seek shelter in the only 'quarter' that has any and have a hot drink and something to eat. After about ten minutes I am joined at the summit by a fellow Pennine Way walker; the first I have met thus far who is walking the whole distance in one go like me. He set off from Edale on Tuesday and is taking 19 days to complete the walk. In conversation it transpires he has completed a number of long distance walks; including the South West Coastal Way and the Cleveland Way.

Our paths continue to cross during the afternoon as we descend Great Shunner Fell and work our way down and round to Keld; where he is staying tonight.

I will be heading on for another five miles beyond Keld to Tan Hill. He tells me that he has also come across a Dutch couple who are also doing the whole distance and who are not far behind us. They may be slower today as the woman got sore feet yesterday on the rocky Cam Road – I know the feeling!

Each time 'Dave' and I pass or one of us catches the other a little more information is gleaned and as I finally arrive in Thwaite I join him outside the café there for a hot drink and a cake. Thwaite is a charming little village and opposite the café and facing back up the way we have come is a very old wooden seat. I wonder how many PW wayfarers have rested there and contemplated their journey.

Most of the descent from the summit; once below the mist and low cloud; has been in fine weather, with the sun making the odd fleeting appearance too. Dave wants to get where he is staying in Keld early enough before, as he puts it, the deluge of coast to coast walkers arrive. He clearly doesn't consider the Coast to Coast to be a proper or challenging enough walk! "It's for a different kind of person" We both agree that you do need to have a good level of fitness to do the Pennine Way. It is during this part of our conversation that he tells me about the helicopter rescue near Standedge last Friday. Apparently just before Wessenden Head; where there is a dip where two streams meet and are negotiated normally without much difficulty; a group of four PW walkers arrived in the afternoon to discover that, after the deluge of rain experienced during the morning and early afternoon, both streams were raging torrents. The group decided that the only way for them to get across was by linking arms and edging sideways to the opposite bank. The power of the water swept them off their feet and though they managed to make the land between the two 'streams', they were all very wet and cold and decided that they couldn't either go forward (across the second torrent) or back from where they were and so contacted the Mountain Rescue service. Once on the scene Mountain Rescue decided that the only way of getting them safely out of their predicament was by summoning a helicopter to hover over the area and lift each in turn. Just goes to show that walking the PW should never be underestimated, not during this summer anyway!

Dave, like me, wasn't aware that you could pick up a certificate from the Old Nag's Head in Edale, which may explain why they were only aware of five people completing the walk so far this year. We continue to catch and pass each other on the pleasant walk from Thwaite to Keld; which in the main follows the contours of the land before descending steeply to a bridge over the river Swale and a rather spectacular waterfall. Keld derives its name from *kelda* – Viking for a spring and was once referred to as "the spring near the apple trees". Swaledale is looking particularly magnificent today. The sun is now completely dominant and I am walking in shorts and just one base layer. A steep climb away from Keld follows and takes me on to a gently rising track along a wall with views of the river and a minor road to my left and long distance views ahead. Near a barn a lapwing starts a frantic circling overhead. I can hear her chicks nearby. I sit and rest for a while by the barn in the lea of the wind, which is by now more of a breeze and nowhere near the strength it was this morning. The rest of the walk to Tan Hill is very pleasant apart from the soggy underfoot conditions. I see a cow with one horn, my does she look silly. I am a mile away from my resting place for the night when the Tan Hill Inn comes into view. It is nice to have a visual goal to reach on the last stretch of a day's walk.

At the Tan Hill Inn I check in and go to my room. At first I can't find the shower, as to access it you have to go into the toilet and shut the door and look behind you. I take off my boots and pack them with paper and then wearily get undressed for a shower. Try as I may I can only get scalding hot water from the shower head and finally give up completely and have to make do with a strip wash, which involves acrobatically getting my feet up into a small sink to get them and my lower legs clean. I also have to use the sink to wash my hair – no hair dryer here either, so it's the good old hand drying technique. Feeling exhausted from my exertions but refreshed and after phone calls from John and from Sandra, I go downstairs for a pint (Golden Sheep) and something to eat. This turns out to be a very tasty homemade lasagne.

Whilst I am drinking the pint and waiting for the food suddenly everyone seems to vacate the pub – is there a fire, is it a drill! It turns out that a sheep is being sheared at the front door of the Inn and everyone has gone out to watch. My camera is upstairs but I do take a picture using my phone. I explain to one of the staff my predicament with the hot water, whereupon a 'friendly lady' offers, with a chuckle, to take me up to my room to 'show me what to do'. Of course she manages to get warm and not scalding water fairly immediately and we laugh and both agree it must have been a 'man thing'.

Back in the bar a group of four bikers come into the pub. They are from Carnforth, three guys, one in his sixties and two in their forties and a woman in her thirties. They have a drink, comment on the view and we exchange pleasantries before they set of home via Hawes. Hawes! – that already seems a long time ago. The jukebox plays 'The sun ain't gonna shine anymore' followed by 'Turn around bright eyes' and I wonder if someone is sending me a message. Either that or the beer is starting to affect my brain. It could of course be the altitude, after all the Tan Hill Inn is the highest pub in the land at 1763feet: maybe I could get the Challenge Committee to come here as part of a Challenge Walk!

As the light outside starts to fade I look out of the window and see a PW signpost about a mile away in the distance – I wonder how many of those I have seen so far on my journey and how many more are yet to come? I am almost tempted to end the evening with a malt whisky, but that honour is reserved for the Border Hotel in 7 days time. I compromise with a half of Butcombe Blonde to sample another beer – a good flavour but the beer is too warm!!

I go to the room and check tomorrow's forecast before turning in for the night. I've got heat from the radiator and can do a little washing and have things dry by morning; as well as ensuring my paper filled boots have every chance of being dry too! It feels strange to be at the half way point of my journey, with, after today, every day being closer to the finish than the start.

DISTANCE WALKED TODAY: 17 MILES

TOTAL DISTANCE WALKED: 133 MILES

CHAPTER TEN

TAN HILL TO MIDDLETON-IN-TEESDALE (Thursday 19th July)

"Hi all, now feeling clean, if tired, after a soak in a hot bath. Weather great today, but conditions underfoot dreadful. First stop in Middleton was at the chemist to stock up on Compeed. May abandon camping on Saturday as I am concerned I won't be able to sort my feet out for the following day. Peter"

I slept fitfully during the night as the bed was not very comfortable, my feet are sore and I end up replacing some Compeed during the night. As I do so I notice a text from Sandra, with a cry for help! It turns out to be a computer problem and as she is desperate to send an e-mail to someone before morning and wanted my help and advice to do so. However by the time I respond the message has been sent. My boots are virtually dry by morning and the washing I draped over the radiator is also dry. I realise why the bed is so uncomfortable as the mattress is only about two inches thick! I was more comfortable in my sleeping bag on a sleeping mat in my tent. I manage to wash my hair under the shower without getting my feet wet. I want to keep them dry for the moment!

Breakfast is ok and I'm off at about five past nine.

The first three and a quarter miles across Sleightholme Moor takes two hours and is the most awful god forsaken terrain I've ever had to negotiate. There is no path, just periodic markers to signify the way; my feet are completely soaked within fifteen minutes of leaving Tan Hill. I can see a fellow PW walker ahead but gradually he disappears as I struggle to make meaningful progress. Looking back the Tan Hill Inn seems still to be very close and I can see two fellow walkers heading in my direction. Later in the day they catch me up and provide companionship as our paths continue to cross for most of the remainder of the walk.

I eventually reach a gravely track near a footbridge and stop to have a drink and take stock. I continue for about two miles now on decent dirt tracks, before once more having to resume walking across desolate country to reach Trough Heads, where I have a choice of continuing ahead to Bowes and a longer route, or bearing left along the main route. As I am heading for Middleton-in-Teesdale it makes sense to take the main route. This turns out to be another section of waterlogged and boggy ground; but my feet can hardly get any wetter, so I carry on and arrive at yet another reservoir and go over a bridge. I am told (by the guide) to go up a bank to my right. After a while of following a path it stops abruptly at a stone wall, which looks as though it was once a stile. I clamber over this and up a steep bracken covered bank to reach a barbed wire fence. A piece of cloth is wrapped tightly round it, suggesting I am not the first walker to have been led this way. I manage to get over it without injury and scramble up a further bank to find the 'real' path again.

I am now heading through boggy wet terrain but I can see the A66 straight ahead, albeit about a mile away. It takes me three-quarters of an hour to get to it. Just before then I cross God's Bridge, a huge natural slab of stone that forms a bridge over the river that flows beneath it. Beyond it is a steep pull up to the road where you walk left and beside it for a while to reach an underpass. Once on the other side there are some rocks where I can stop and sit for a while and have a rest and some lunch. The two other walkers I had seen earlier in the day catch me up at this point. They also stayed at the Tan Hill last night and as it turns out are heading for the same B&B in Middleton-in-Teesdale as I am.

Throughout the remainder of the day our paths continue to cross as I later catch them up when they have stopped for lunch and much later they catch me again when I am taking a break. One started the PW on Wednesday, the day before me and the other joined him at Hawes. He had previously walked the PW from Edale to Hawes – they are now both walking the whole way together.

After leaving the A66 I have a second encounter with a lapwing clearly guarding its nearby nest. As I stand to try and take a picture of it, she dive bombs me. I do however manage to take a snap of her as she circles above me calling frantically. Many times during the day I debate with myself about stopping to change into dry socks, but the guide describes the next bit as 'boggy' (and that's not written from the perspective of the wettest summer on record) so I know that if that is the case the 'dry' socks will be as wet as those they have replaced in no time at all. I eventually stop about a mile and a half from Middleton, confident that there is no more boggy ground for the rest of today's walk and I sort out my feet and finally put dry socks on – what a relief!

I arrive at Middleton-in-Teesdale and just catch the chemist before they close and take their complete stock of Compeed (four packs) – life saver! I find the B&B and the landlady is expecting me as my two fellow walkers had surged ahead after my 'foot stop' and had heralded my imminent arrival. I leave my boots in the hall and go up to my room which is very spacious and I have my own separate private bathroom with a bath!! It is not long before I am soaking in it turning the water a mucky colour as my legs are filthy. After a good soak I get dry and sort out my feet. Whenever I have used Compeed before it normally stays in place and remains effective despite bathing or showering, for several days. However I am finding walking with constantly wet feet means each plaster has to be changed, at least once every other day.

Middleton is a small market town that was expanded in the early nineteenth century, when the London Lead Company moved its headquarters there. It is said to have early links to the co-operative movement that predate even the 'Rochdale Pioneers'. So once I am dressed I go out in search of the local Co-op and purchase a sandwich for tomorrow's packed lunch and buy a paper. Back at the B&B I skim read it and most of it gets used to stuff my boots. There is plenty left over for my two fellow PW travellers too. I speak to Sandra, text my daughters and send off my daily text to those following my progress.

As my feet are still rather tender and there is a hotel next to the B&B that does food and has cask ales, deciding where to go for a meal is easily resolved. I have a very good pint of Rivet Catcher and a wonderful slow roasted brisket, one of my favourites. It is rather expensive, but I feel I have earned it today. I had been to Middleton before and had forgotten just how 'high brow' and 'twee' elements of it were. Both barmaids were very pleasant, though certainly no description of either of them would contain the words high brow or 'twee'. I followed the brisket with a cheeseboard which was heavenly as well!

The background music was good too; firstly tracks from Coldplay's - XYZ and then from Snow Patrol's - Eyes Open. These albums were then followed by a selection of music starting with one from Dusty Springfield – 'the white queen of soul'.

It turns out that the Barmaid, who serves me my food, is in to Coldplay and Snow Patrol too and we share experiences as we have both seen them live. She is probably in her twenties and I am old enough to be her father at best; yet good music has no age barriers and she is positively beaming at sharing stories with me. I pay the bill and again find myself sharing music stories, this time with both barmaids. I am inwardly singing and feeling very contented as I leave the hotel and then have a shock as it is absolutely bucketing it down outside. I'm glad I have only next door to go to.

I don't sleep very well and realise during the night that the bedclothes include a quilt, a throw and a cover. I get rid of the latter two and get some sleep. I am instantly awake when I hear a clock in the house strike eight o'clock; it turns out to be half an hour fast thankfully.

DISTANCE WALKED TODAY: 17 MILES

TOTAL DISTANCE WALKED: 150 MILES

CHAPTER ELEVEN

MIDDLETON-IN-TEESDALE TO DUFTON (Friday 20th July)

"Hi all, Best day so far, dry pleasant walking, great scenery, waterfalls and cliffs. Some scrambling, going slightly off piste and fording a river. Feet held up well. Am now booked in a B&B tomorrow night. Tomorrow is the high stuff over Cross Fell. Peter"

I enjoy breakfast with my two PW companions and it turns out in conversation that they are staying at the same B&B as I am in Dufton tonight. They leave before me but are heading first to the Co-op to purchase a sandwich for their lunch. After I leave the B&B I ring Sandra and explain that I am a little concerned about camping wild tomorrow night, in terms of being able to get my feet washed and sorting out my blisters. I ask if she wouldn't mind seeing if she could book me a B&B in Alston as an alternative. I have a pleasant stroll down the road to rejoin the PW and then take a very enjoyable walk along a path through fields and meadows that is never very far from the river Tees until after about 3 miles Low Force is reached.

So far today's walk has taken an hour and twenty minutes. It is a further mile and a half to High Force and both falls are in spectacular states because of all the recent rain; there is no rain today though and that makes a welcome change. I am in, and will remain in, tee shirt and shorts for the whole of today's walk.

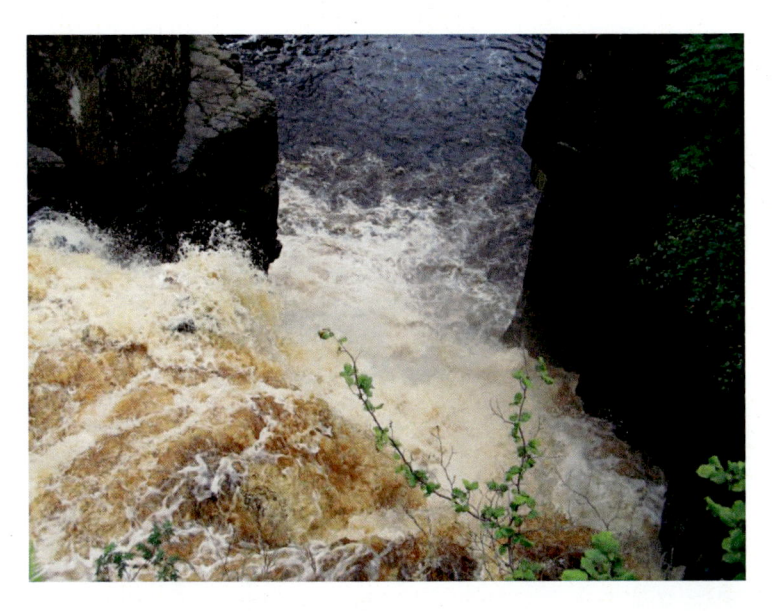

After leaving High Force the route deviates away from the river as it climbs gentle rolling hills and moors before rejoining it. I can now see my two fellow PW walkers in my sights ahead. I also pass a fisherman deep in the river fly fishing and as I near he has a bite and lands a thrashing salmon about a foot long into his keep net. The, for once, pleasant path then gives way to boulders along the rivers edge and I enjoy scrambling from one to the next and eventually catch my two PW travellers just as the foaming torrents of Cauldron Snout can be heard ahead. Cauldron Snout is indeed spectacular today with the foaming peaty waters being squeezed between rocks as they tumble downwards towards me. I am exhilarated by more scrambling up to some rocks adjacent to the first cascade of water and midge repellent applied; enjoy my lunch- courtesy of both the Co-op in Middleton and my ever available, but now dwindling supply of goodies. It is about 1.30pm and my lunch spot represents the half way point of today's walk.

My two companions find an adjacent rock from which to eat their lunch and after a short while the three of us leave the foaming waters of Cauldron Snout together and head off for the long cross country stretch to High Cup Nick. As we pass a farm and head out into open country the path gets boggy again and although nothing compared with yesterday, suddenly my boots are wet once more. I am following slightly behind my two PW 'comrades' and not really paying as much attention as I should be doing to our route, as we are sticking to what appears to be the only path in town. I am also watching where my feet go to protect them as best I can. Suddenly I catch up with my companions as they have stopped to work out where we are as the path seems to suddenly disappear altogether. Following a consultation with his GPS, Trevor (as I later find out) indicates that we are on a parallel route to the PW path but about 100metres higher up and away from where the 'true' path appears to be indicated on the map.

We head down to the river, which is a tributary of the Tees and agree that in relation to where we are we should have crossed the river at a bridge further down stream; back in the direction we have come from; and be on a path we can now see on the other side of the river.

We each set off to find a fording point and I find one that involves lots of boulder hopping and make it across to the other side. Trevor and Paul have gone down stream and I signal to them that I have found a route across and they head back towards where I am. Trevor doesn't like the look of it and carries on up stream; whilst Paul negotiates his way across to join me. Trevor then returns and also fords the river in the same place, although he manages to put a foot in the water on his way across.

The three of us then head off together towards High Cup Nick on a clearer and much better footpath. High Cup Nick is as spectacular as I remember it from my last visit with Jed; a great border collie of mine; who is sadly no longer with us. Both Trevor and Paul are impressed too as we head along the edge of one side of the feature, with its huge and yet elegant rock buttresses and its green hollowed out glacial valley beyond.

I stop to rest, have a drink and a biscuit and Trevor and Paul go on. As well as stopping at the same B&B tonight I am now aware of their planned itinerary for the rest of the walk. They are going as far as Garrigill tomorrow and then taking two days to cover the distance I will cover from Alston in one day. They will catch me up again at Byrness, but are taking an extra day to cover the last stretch to Kirk Yetholm and so will finish the walk the day after me.

As I finish my drink and pack the flask away I turn on my phone and have a signal and laugh out loud when I see a text from Sandra. She has found me accommodation for Saturday night at Garrigill at the same B&B that Trevor and Paul are staying. Firstly they will now think I am dogging there footsteps – I had shared with them my proposed route for the rest of the journey too. Secondly Garrigill is four miles before Alston and will now mean I have a long 28 mile walk to complete on Sunday. I share this information with Trevor and Paul when I catch them up again on the long descent into Dufton, including the fact that our paths are going to continue to remain in step for a little longer on our PW journey. It is at this point that I initiate introductions and now we are all on first name terms.

Arriving in Dufton we walk through the whole village looking for our B&B, which turns out to be half a mile beyond it. I am told by the landlady to go round the back, where I have my own separate room / facilities; whilst Trevor and Paul are directed to the other side of the building. I take off my boots and stuff them with what remains of the newspaper I bought in Middleton yesterday and then have a shower and once again sort out my feet. As it is a warm and pleasant evening I wash some walking socks and peg them onto a washing line and leave my boots outside in the sun too. I set off back to the village to get something to eat at the pub and manage to combine the act of walking with compiling my daily text to my 'followers'.

As the only watering hole and it being a Friday evening the Stag Inn is very busy. I manage to find a table and head for the bar and whilst there Paul and Trevor arrive and I get a round in. We ask for menus to order food;

another very tasty and satisfying lasagne for me. I enjoy a pint of Skiddaw followed by a pint of Eden Gold. Both are good and I settle the tab and leave Trevor and Paul, who stay on to sink a few more beers.

Back at Coneygarth I bring in the boots and retrieve the socks from the line. Today has been a very special and enjoyable day, the best day of the PW so far. Curlew, snipe, oyster catcher, dippers, yellow hammers and thrushes have all shared part of my journey and 'said their piece' during the day. The weather has been dry and warm for the most part and the scenery, especially the waterfalls and High Cup Nick have been great too. Tomorrow is now a shorter day (16miles) because I am staying at Garrigill, but this will mean a 28mile walk on Sunday – Oh well!

DISTANCE WALKED TODAY: 21 MILES

TOTAL DISTANCE WALKED: 171 MILES

CHAPTER TWELVE

DUFTON TO GARRIGILL (Saturday 21st July)

"Hi all, No signal here at garrigill so you may not get this update till Sunday. Sunny day but cooler above 2000ft, which is where we were for most of it. Knock Fell, Great Dunn Fell, Little Dunn Fell and Cross Fell all summited today. Long walk tomorrow to Twice Brewed. Peter"

At breakfast a fourth guest of the B&B is revealed; a woman who is doing the PW in stages. She started in her twenties with mainly 'day' walks and now after her children are older, she is seeking to finish it. She is today setting off for Garrigill (but staying in a different B&B to Trevor, Paul and me) and then has two more days to get to Greenhead. She lives in York and hopes to finish the Greenhead to Kirk Yetholm stretch in five days. She is the first to leave and tells us all she is a very slow walker! After breakfast I retire to my 'quarters' to finish packing and set off, not sure whether I am off before Trevor and Paul or whether they have already left.

I walk up the village, past the pub where we spent an enjoyable evening yesterday and regain the PW. It is a pleasant start to the day, being warm and sunny. I go past a derelict farm at Halsteads and reflect that this must be the fifth or sixth such farm that I have past during my journey to date. My route is taking me between a pleasant avenue of trees along a slightly rising path that has lots of tree roots and muddy patches that I need to beware of. It isn't long however before I leave the trees behind and a long straight track rises steeply in front of me to a gate in the far distance. I resolve to get to the gate before taking a breather and manage to do this albeit perspiring a little by the time I arrive at the gate. I have a drink and a quick rest; looking back I see Paul and Trevor just starting up the climb.

I go through the gate and almost immediately have to negotiate a second gate, where I am faced by a herd of cows and a bull and also have a stream to cross, either side of which has been churned up by the hooves of my four legged companions.

The guide indicates that the path swings left, so once across the stream I stay lower down crossing marshy ground with clumps of bull rushes, gorse and heather obscuring any path that may or may not have been present. After continuing for a while I am sure that I am not following any path at all and recheck the map and scan the landscape for recognisable features to try and locate my 'route'. I backtrack and climb higher up to my right, to where I believe I should be and eventually do find the PW path again.

I have probably lost about five minutes during this excursion and now face a steep climb up to Swindale Beck, where the path drops down to a footbridge to cross the swirling waters of the Beck and then rises very steeply up to my right. The Swindale flows north-eastwards through Bampton before joining the River Lowther. The Lowther is a tributary of the River Eamont, which in turn is a tributary of the River Eden, which then flows into the Solway Firth near Carlisle.

I resolve to tackle this next steep stage by walking for 500 paces before having a rest, after a short while this 'target' gets reduced to 200, but I then manage to keep going for 250 paces before taking a well earned 5 minute break for a drink and a bite to eat. I can see Paul and Trevor, much closer to me now as they head up from Swindale Beck.

I wait for them to 'catch up' and we exchange greetings, before I set off again and leave them to 'catch their breath' too! I need one further stop on the climb before arriving at a very prominent cairn that has been tantalisingly on the horizon for the last fifteen minutes. This is described as the 'Old Man of Knock' and is a sturdy well made cairn, which on one side has a sheep's skull embedded within it. This provides a weird and very macabre backdrop for a picture of Trevor and Paul as they join me and the Old Man.

The summit cairn of Knock Fell is further on and not as prominent. From here however and until we arrive there, we have great views of the giant football and tall masts that are the Civil Aviation Authority's air traffic control radar station that adorns Great Dunn Fell, which is the next summit the PW will visit. The giant summit radomes are visible for about forty miles around and for some are real intrusions on the landscape.

I have always viewed them with a kind of affection; either when driving up or down the M6 or when passing them by train on the Settle to Carlisle line.

From Knock Fell the route drops down to a tarmac road, which is the highest such road in the country, as it winds its way up to the summit plateau of Great Dunn Fell. It services the radar station and we follow it for a little while before the PW veers off to the right and climbs the shoulder of the mountain. It takes us to just below the Radar Station and the summit, as we pass by and head towards the next peak in this, the highest section of the Pennine Chain.

Our path to and over Little Dunn Fell and then on to Cross Fell, the highest point of the Pennines, is clearly visible ahead, as in the distance is the fourth member of our morning breakfast table. The path drops down again first before a steep pull takes us on to the summit of Little Dunn Fell, no pause this time as I carry on up the last major climb of the day to the Cross Fell summit plateau. During this ascent I pass and catch our fellow B&B guest and finally reach another prominent cairn, which marks the start of a gentler rise to the summit trig point and the cross shelter beyond it.

It is quite busy on top, but Trevor, Paul and I manage to find one quarter of the shelter 'free' and get some respite from the wind and enjoy some lunch, with lovely views of the Eden Valley below us and the Lakeland fells on the horizon. Our fellow breakfaster arrives, but carries on without stopping after a brief hello. We are half way to Garrigill and it has taken until 1.15pm to get to the summit (four hours twenty minutes to cover some eight or nine miles).

It is now going to be a long drag to Garrigill. The route, the 'Corpse Road' lives up to its name, it is relentless, dropping down at first at right angles from the summit of Cross Fell to meet a cross path, west to east over the Pennines from the Eden Valley to our left. I remember coming up from the Eden Valley side to climb Cross Fell some 25 years earlier and getting to the summit in mist and low cloud with no views at all. Cross Fell is not only special in being the highest point of the Pennines, it also has its own micro climate when the wind is coming from the north east (as it was earlier in my journey). *However today it is blowing from the more usual south-westerly direction.* The great wind it produces on these occasions can be of hurricane proportions and is experienced in the Eden Valley to its west. It is known as the Helm Wind and can strike most unexpectedly, usually during the spring. A long time ago the Fell was called Fiends Fell, as it was thought to be haunted and home to malevolent spirits and in 1586 a cross was erected on the summit in an attempt to banish them. Perhaps that is why our fellow female breakfaster didn't want to hang around!

As we leave the summit and are on our descent to the cross path it appears, maybe in her haste to avoid the 'fiends', that our lady walker has gone the wrong way on reaching it. However, before we get to the cross path we see her back track, although she is now, of course, behind us again. After about a mile eastwards along the cross track we arrive at Greg's Hut, a place of refuge in bad weather. Trevor, Paul and I are walking together at this point and the hut provides another photo opportunity and a chance to peek inside too. As we are doing this our lady companion catches up, but clearly doesn't want to join us as she hangs back to 'explore' Greg's' Hut on her own as we set off on the long descent again.

The going is often hard and rocky underfoot, which I suppose does make a change from waterlogged and boggy ground. It does however not take long before I have to be careful in which part of my foot makes contact with the ground so as not to aggravate further any tender spots. A welcome break from the tedium of this stretch is a telephone call from my brother in France, as he seeks to catch up with my progress. Trevor and Paul forge ahead again at this point and I do stop about a mile before Garrigill, partly to have a drink and also to give my feet a rest from their pounding.

The B&B turns out to be somewhat primitive. It is also the post office and village store and is right next door to the pub – its most redeeming feature. It has a shared bathroom and Paul and Trevor are the only other guests. I think I manage to persuade the landlady to do breakfast for me at 7.45am, because she has the Sunday papers to deliver before then. If I can get away by 8am I might have a chance of getting to the Twice Brewed Inn by 8pm tomorrow evening. After a shower and the usual ritual now of sorting out my feet – two new blisters have emerged during the day's walk – I go up to the lounge. Paul is trying to get the huge silver TV screen to work. Together we manage to do this and watch a few minutes of the Open Golf, before Trevor joins us and the three of us head next door to the pub, where we meet Gary; who was also at the Tan Hill and Susan; our mystery walker from the B&B at Dufton and whose path we have crossed several times today.

A good session of pleasant banter ensues about the Pennine Way, walking and other such matters and in between all this we order food and have one or two rounds of drinks. I enjoy a very hearty steak and ale pie plus three and a half pints of Allendale's Golden Plover – very drinkable. The pub is apparently under new management, although for 'new' read 'old'.

One member of the clientele stands out too during our stay. He has clearly had one too many and he becomes very loud at times. He does however come out with some memorable and completely out of context one liners; "don't stand on the brown mushroom". It appears he is also a Sunderland fan, as in his 'well oiled' state he shouts out that "he thinks they (Sunderland) may have won something once". I take down Paul's e-mail address, so that if I do manage to translate my daily scribblings into the story of my journey I can send it to him. He will then forward it on to Trevor. The Tan Hill comes in for quite a pasting in some way or other from all apart from Susan, who apparently had a very pleasant experience when she stayed there a couple of years ago.

It is Susan who leaves first but I am not long after, leaving Paul, Trevor and Gary to continue the banter. I draft my text to the 'usual suspects' although there is no signal at the B&B and it may not get to everyone before tomorrow. I finish writing my notes of the day. Apart from the long descent from Cross Fell and the hammering to my feet, it has been a rather splendid day all round.

The B&B is like the house that time forgot, with outdated décor, basic furnishings and tired knick-knacks competing with liberally scattered notices about what guests can and cannot do. The hairdryer in the room is about ten years old, was probably the cheapest model on the market in its day and has melted and reformed into new shapes. I use it with trepidation, but it works. The room is stepped up into from a corridor that has my room and the bathroom on one side and the hosts bedroom and the room that Trevor has on the other side.

The door is set about three feet into the room, but flush to the internal walls, which were painted in a bright orange colour some years before, only the brushing didn't quite reach the ceiling and did spill over onto the skirting board and the beading round the door opening. The carpet is kind of matted shagpile, the exact colour of which it is difficult to discern. The room itself has a narrow single bed on one side of which is a bedside cabinet that won't open. This has a lamp on it. On the other side of the bed is a white mdf set of drawers with a mirror placed at the back. There are two cut glass vases in the room each stuffed with artificial flowers. To one side of the door is a precariously leaning mdf shelf on which a tray, a kettle and the usual tea making facilities are perched.

When I negotiate my way into the bed it feels like it must be the smallest single bed ever designed, not helped by the fact that the covers are so tightly drawn around it that it feels like I am getting back into my sleeping bag again. Well I was supposed to be under canvas tonight! However remarkably enough I sleep ok, with only one nocturnal visit to the adjacent facilities.

I am awoken at 5.30am however by the sound of rain, which is soon over with and the sound of knocking on the front door. Apparently either Paul or Trevor had left the key in the lock when they returned from the pub, which meant the paper delivery man couldn't access the building to leave the Sunday papers, so had needed to knock up our hostess to gain entry.

I am now wide awake and on checking my watch to see the time I find in the only drawer of any piece of furniture I manage to open a copy of the Pennine Way Association Newsletter. The PWA it turns out is a registered charity and the newsletter has articles written by people who had walked the PW. I resolve to find out more about the Association on my return home.

DISTANCE WALKED TODAY: 16 MILES

TOTAL DISTANCE WALKED: 187 MILES

CHAPTER THIRTEEN

GARRIGILL TO TWICE BREWED (Sunday 22nd July)

"Hi all, Hell of a day, attacked by a cow, lost the trail twice, got bawled at by a farmer, had to negotiate two golf courses, up to my knees in wet boggy stuff, climbed the highest point along Hadrian's Wall and was on the go for 13 hours: and that's probably only half the story. Now have Trevor for company for the last 3 days. Only 60 miles to go. Peter"

I get up and get ready for my long day ahead and as I am leaving the room to use the bathroom encounter the landlady who quizzes me about who was last back from the pub and explains about the reason for the early morning disturbance. Apparently there is a host as well as a hostess and he has gone to deliver the papers on his own, so I am now offered the opportunity of an earlier breakfast and agree to dine at 7.15am. This turns out to be very nice indeed – the best bacon so far on the trip. Trevor comes down to wish me well at 7.45 as I am readying for the off. I won't see him and Paul again until Byrness in two days time.

It feels very pleasant walking out of Garrigill and then along the river. Initially I have an early morning dog walker for company and then for about a mile my 'companion' becomes a curlew, regularly sharing its call. The path then takes me across a footbridge and a rather overgrown and waterlogged section follows, with the map and guide indicating I should keep left. After about ten minutes negotiating this terrain I am clearly not on the PW and have to back track until I spot a signpost further up and to my right. Having regained the route I am dismayed to discover that within five minutes it has disappeared again. I am following a clear footpath and I follow the footpath sign, which takes me into and through a farm. I have to contend with a snarly dog as I go through the first gate into the yard that weaves round a number of farm buildings into a field with a collection of rusting farm machinery and a number of sheep.

The path appears to continue to a gate into a field containing a number of lambs all about six months old. Lambs for the slaughter I suspect! I have barely gone twenty metres into the field beyond the gate when a shouting farmer tells me I am not on the footpath. I retrace my steps and he points out where a gate stile in the wall at one side of the first field provides my exit from the farm. I pat him on the back and thank him for his assistance. He assures me that once through the gate stile I should follow the path round the golf course.

Once I am through the gate and on the golf course I find that there is no evident path in either direction so I have to decide whether to follow the course round to my right or to my left. I decide to head right but after a short while and on re-consulting the map decide that I would be nearer to the PW if I was on the left hand-side of the course. There are no golfers out at this time of the morning and I head down and across the course until I reach the other side of the course. I carry on following the edge of the course for a short while and then find I have to negotiate a barbed wire fence with a steep drop down on the other side to gain a clearly defined track. I take off the rucksack and lower it gingerly down on the other side catching the mesh of a pocket as I do so. It takes me a little while to 'unhook' the sack from the fence and finally I and all my belongings are free of the golf course at last.

In my haste to put this experience behind me I head right along the track, but quickly realise that this is taking me further away from where the 'real PW' is hiding. Having rechecked my bearings and retraced my steps down hill I reach another track and turn right along it. I can now work out exactly where I am and am on a footpath that runs parallel with the PW all the way to Alston. I decide that rather than trying to negotiate more open country down a slope and go through trees to rejoin the 'official' route, it might be sensible to stick to my current path. This takes me past a rather nice house which is for sale and then over a stile into a field in which I am confronted by two llamas, who appear to be all teeth and look rather menacing. However I get through the field and through another farmyard and from there to Alston I am on a tarmac track. Once in Alston I get some cash from a 'hole in the wall' and head down towards the station.

Having lost time over the first four miles of my day; it has taken me two hours to cover them; I decide to follow what the guide describes as the 'alternative PW option'. The South Tyne Railway in its heyday connected Alston to the industry and sea ports of the North East. About five miles of the track from Alston has now been reclaimed and a little steam train now travels up and down this stretch. I pass the sheds where volunteers are preparing a brightly coloured blue engine for its first trip of the day (in about an hour's time).

The decision to follow the South Tyne Trail which runs alongside the track is a good one. This change of plan, coupled with the presence of a clear and level path to follow, make for a very interesting walk as I go under bridges and am able to take in the scenery to either side of the railway. I follow the Trail for about 6 miles and the stretch only takes me a further 2 hours. I also find my third long and distinctive feather of the walk and decide to store this one in a side pocket of the rucksack for safe keeping, rather than in my map case.

The rest of the walk along the PW to Greenhead is along a path that at times is indistinct and at times is nonexistent. It dumps me over the top of stiles into 'lakes' and endless quagmires. It takes me across stretches which the guide itself describes as a 'squelchy quagmire' – after the summer we have had this is like wading through six inches of muddy water. After reaching one point whilst crossing Hartleyburn Common and yet again having nothing under my feet to call a path I consult the map and guide to work out which direction to head in. The only option is to find the most distinguishing feature in the landscape in the general direction I am headed and take a compass bearing and just keep heading along it. I do this for about a mile and

I arrive within five metres of where I should be; a fact that lifts my spirits.

I am now following a section where the guide suggests it is important to stick to the footpath (if you can see it) 'no matter how many times it meanders'. It is sodden, squelchy and at times well over the boots. However it is also clear that to either side; as my trusty walking pole testifies; the depths I would sink to would be considerably further. Eventually I arrive at a ladder stile about twenty metres to the right of a trig point, which is on the other side of the wall. The trig point is at 948 feet, but isn't visited. I am now on the boggy moor-land of Blenkinsop Common.

At one point; I remember consulting my watch and it being three thirty; whilst crossing the common I get to a house and the route takes me past a number of cars, some of which don't appear to have been moved for a number of years. A man appears from the house and I am offered water if I need it and reassured that it is only five miles to Greenhead. I decline the offer of water and thank him for the information. Another five miles for today would be great, It's a pity therefore that I am going seven miles beyond Greenhead, though I don't share this fact with him. As I climb another ladder stile to leave the track at the back of the property I am confronted by what can only be described as a small lake. For at least ten metres in all directions all I have to step into and cross is water. After initially trying to pick the shallowest route I give up and wade across to reach squelchy mud again.

After another hour of negotiating similar conditions I seem to be finally leaving the boggy wilderness behind and the route takes me to a gate and swings right across a large field where I can see cows and sheep a plenty. The clear track goes straight ahead now and four hundred metres ahead I can see that the 'kind' farmer has dumped a feeding trough right in the middle of it. A number of the cows are indeed feeding from the trough; there are also calves around too. I approach with caution tapping my stick on the ground as I do so and some cows shy away from the trough, but several don't and I alter my route to veer right of the path to avoid them. As I do this and suddenly without warning a cow that is ahead of me and to my right turns and charges at speed straight for me!

What a way for my PW journey to end – 'he always wanted to walk the PW but he was stopped in his tracks and squashed by a two and a half ton cow two miles from Greenhead' – was the inscription I imagined on my tombstone. I waved and thrashed my stick on the ground frantically and the cow continued until within three feet of me she suddenly veered away snorting as she did so. I could almost hear the pounding of my heart as I gathered myself, quickened my pace and didn't dare to look back as I headed for a gate further on and breathed a sigh of relief when I was on the other side of it.

The track now veers down to the left as I head straight for the A68 and then have to negotiate four lanes of traffic to find the PW on the other side. The next section of the walk adds new interest as it joins the Hadrian's Wall walk and I admit I do stop to take the odd picture or two. I see a solitary buzzard soaring on the thermals above the wall. Not surprisingly the path is very up and down as it follows the wall which runs west to east more or less in a straight line. I had confirmed to Trevor having crossed the A68 that I expected to be at Twice Brewed at between 7.45 and 8pm and soon realise that, because of the frequent climbs and descents that are slowing my progress; and possibly my picture taking; this is going to be a challenge.

The last section of the day's walk sees me climb the highest point of Hadrian's Wall before dropping down to the road that will take me to the Twice Brewed Hotel. Trevor and Christine are waiting for me when I finally get there at 8.15pm. I am able to let go of the tent, the sleeping bag, sleeping mat, pillow and four of my OS maps, so tomorrow my 'load' will be much lighter. Trevor has ordered our meal for about 8.45pm, so I quickly go up to the room and then find the shower to get clean, dry and changed, which is an effort. Eventually I rejoin Trevor at exactly 8.45, Christine has already set off on her return journey to Whitley Bay, and the food arrives on cue and is quickly followed by a welcome pint. Indeed we enjoy a few beers before retiring.

I got to know Trevor and Christine, through visiting our daughter and grand daughter in Whitley Bay. Sandra first met Christine through a knitting group and Trevor and I were 'fixed up', by our partners, to go out for a pint. As a result of this on the occasions when I would be staying overnight in Whitley Bay we would make arrangements to meet. Trips to the pub became a regular feature of my visits to the area, as we found we had a lot in common; in particular a great love of sport. Trevor has been in to athletics most of his life and still competes as a 'vet'. He had run marathons in the past and since I started running some twelve years ago I have completed twelve.

We also shared a love of good real ale too. I was a little sceptical when 'Trev' suggested he might walk the last three days with me, as although he was fit enough to indulge in field event athletics; hammer throwing, shot and even pole vaulting; he hadn't done a lot of fell walking. I also suspected that the reputation for a good range of real ales at the Twice Brewed Inn, might be the real attraction.

I do get off to sleep almost straight away, but am awake in the early hours as my feet are paining me; I just can't seem to get them in a comfortable position. At this point I realise that Trevor is awake too and the room is very stuffy. We open a window for some fresh air, which makes it more bearable. I sleep fitfully for the rest of the night.

DISTANCE WALKED TODAY: 28 MILES

TOTAL DISTANCE WALKED: 215 MILES

CHAPTER FOURTEEN

TWICE BREWED TO BELLINGHAM (Monday 23rd July)

"Hi all, Another hard but enjoyable day. Hot sunshine and strong winds. Now at Bellingham, only two more days to go. Peter"

Breakfast is largely self–service but very good. It is surprising how many people are staying at the hotel and how big it is, considering its miles from anywhere. We are ready to set off just after nine am. I retrace the steps to Hadrian's Wall, where I left the PW yesterday evening; but now have Trevor as a companion.

Back at the 'Wall' we head east and again experience lots of ups and downs and some good photo opportunities. Trevor quickly realises that the PW is not just a 'stroll in the park' and a long term knee injury means that he cannot climb the hills as quickly as I can, nor can he descend without protecting the suspect knee. This involves leading with the wrong leg and means that the down stretches are even more challenging than the ups.

However we eventually reach and pass Milecastle 39 and one final climb and descent leads us to the end of our 'love affair' with the wall as the PW heads due north away from it. This provides for some difficult underfoot terrain again and I do well to keep my feet dry.

We then enter a wooded area with squelchy boggy paths to follow. At times it is a challenge keeping to the driest part of the path, whilst restraining the branches of adjacent trees from knocking us over. The wind is picking up again and as the day wears on the sun gets hotter and hotter and eventually it is the challenge of both the wind and sun that take precedent over the challenge of the terrain we are crossing. We drop down to cross a stream and see a home-made sign that promises refreshments in one mile. A little further on as we are about to scramble up a steep bank a further sign proclaims; 'Refreshments at the top of the hill' 'Beware of the Bull'.

Luckily the bull is occupied in another part of the field and as we finally reach the top of the hill and a farmhouse at Horneystead. We go through a gate to our left, where a picnic table and chairs are laid out for us. The refreshments are of the do-it-yourself variety, with a price list and an honesty box. There are tea and coffee making facilities and a small fridge containing milk and cold drinks. There is also a book for people to write in their comments too. There are plastic containers with descriptions on them; biscuits, scones etc. However, the one proclaiming to contain home-made scones is empty.

I read in the book that a party of one adult and two children travelling north to south (because they live near Edale) and whom we passed and spoke to about two miles back, found them particularly delicious. Ah well a biscuit and a cup of tea are very refreshing too. I think Trevor is particularly happy to have time for a break from the rigours of the PW. We also have the attention of a very friendly cat to amuse us too.

The day also connects us to other PW walkers; a lady and her husband – she did it many years ago but is now taking her time to do it again – they stayed at the Twice Brewed Hotel last night and will be staying in Bellingham tonight too. She tells me about purchasing an expensive pair of waterproof socks in Alston, but confirms that they are effective. We also meet a father and son, the latter in his early teens, who are also heading to Bellingham. Soon after leaving our 'refreshment' stop we are faced with a challenge of crossing fields where there is no clear path and we have to pick out stiles/gates in walls or fences and head towards them.

This is all very well but the third stile in this sequence is 'guarded' by two horses and it is only with some considerable patience and gentle persuasion that we coax them to move sufficiently to allow us to scale the stile. We cross the next field to a farm, where a barking dog makes sure we don't dally too long as it literally 'dogs' our footsteps. In the next field we are glared at by a flock of larger than usual sheep and I start to think that all the animals along the PW are in contact with one another and are 'programmed' to create additional challenges to my progress. Even Trevor finds it strange that we are encountering such a variety of livestock and how menacing some of them seem to be.

When Trevor decided he would join me for the last four nights and three days of my walk I had already booked overnight accommodation at each stopping off point. He had managed to confirm reservations at three of the four, including last nights, however tonight he had had to find us a different B&B, as the place I had booked could not accommodate him too. Ironically all of our fellow travellers heading for Bellingham were staying at the B&B I had previously booked.

Our route now takes us on a succession of ups and downs as we cross field after field and cross lots of marshy ground. We come to the very attractive house and gardens of Lowstead and follow its access track. Eventually we arrive at a minor road and spend about thirty minutes walking on tarmac, the longest stretch so far. Eventually we leave the tarmac and are back on moor land again and have a steep pull that takes us up towards a mast on Ealingham Rigg, with a bunkhouse to our left.

After following a clear track we then again have indistinct paths to negotiate as we cross more boggy heath land.

Finally we have a view of Bellingham in the distance. Trevor is now really struggling and I begin to get concerned about whether in joining me for these three days he has bitten off more than he can chew and also whether I may need to rethink the planned itinery as a consequence. As ever on a day's walk the last mile is always the longest and it seems to take ages as we continue along the road to Bellingham and then along by the river before we emerge into the town centre.

Bellingham is a bustling market town that nestles alongside the River North Tyne and has a number of shops, café's and B&B's; plus three pubs; only the one of which was open when we arrived. It is known as the gateway to Kielder Forest and Kielder Water and is probably the largest town I have encountered since Alston.

During the day Trevor had informed me that our digs for the night are about a mile out of Bellingham itself, so we agree to have a pint at the first pub we come to before deciding on our next move. It is ten past six and the first pub we come to doesn't open until 6.30pm. I go for a wander and find a second pub that isn't open yet either. Finally I find a third, 'The Cheviot' which is open and persuade Trevor to walk a further 50 metres. It is well worth it as we enjoy a very nice pint there and decide to eat at The Cheviot before finding our digs.

We meet the couple who stayed at Twice Brewed last night and the man and his son and later on to my surprise Trevor and Paul arrive too. I hadn't expected to see them until Byrness. They had stayed at Greenhead last night, so had had a 21 mile day followed by today's 22 miles, whereas my 28 miles to Twice Brewed had been followed by today's 15 miles. The meal is good and I am feeling well fed and somewhat refreshed. At 7.45pm Trevor rings our B&B and tells our hostess that we are ok and have decided to eat in Bellingham before heading there. She suggests that she should pick us up from The Cheviot at 8pm and drive us to the B&B. Trevor readily accepts her kind offer.

When we get to the B&B it is a really pleasant surprise. Whilst it has been a farmhouse it has been modernised and extended and has modern decor, large rooms; the en suite to our room is for example bigger than the bedroom I had at Garrigill. We have a lounge with a TV in it and another room with tea and coffee making facilities. Barbara (as we later discover is the name of our hostess) brings us a pot of tea and readily agrees to do some washing and drying for me. She is also happy to drive us back to Bellingham in the morning, so that we can pick up the PW again. It is a beautiful house with well manicured and mature gardens overlooking the river. Barbara also has some holiday lets which she has operated for 10 years, but only started doing Bed and Breakfast as well after taking early retirement some two years ago. This is definitely the best B&B so far. After showering and attention to my feet I am able to catch up on my daily log.

The beds are really comfortable too and I enjoy the best night's sleep of the whole PW journey. The quality and comfort of the B&B is second to none so far and I wake refreshed at 6.10am. It is grey and misty and a fine light drizzle is falling. I watch a rabbit meander across the well manicured lawn and disappear into a deep border filled with a host of flowers and bushes. Further down past the end of the lawn, the dark river flows silently past. Even in poor weather this is a beautiful spot.

DISTANCE WALKED TODAY: 15 MILES

TOTAL DISTANCE WALKED: 230 MILES

CHAPTER FIFTEEN

BELLINGHAM TO BYRNESS (Tuesday 24th July)

"Hi all, Arrived at Byrness at 6. A day of varying challenges that at times was fun. Mist and drizzly rain for the first 4 hours. Had to navigate round obstacles, leave and rejoin the PW, have one of the worst boggy areas to contend with and finish with a 6mile walk through Kielder Forest. One final long day tomorrow. What a fascinating journey it has been. Peter"

When I get downstairs for breakfast I find all my clothes washed and dried and neatly placed in a pile. We start breakfast at 8am; the best of the week, there is not an ounce of grease on the plate. Barbara apologizes for the size of the bacon. She is sourcing it from a local rare breed pig farmer. It might be small but there are four rashers and it is very tasty. The breakfast table is laid as if we were staying in an upmarket five star hotel, with china teacups and linen serviettes rolled up in silver rings. It is a breakfast experience to savour. Barbara's house is immaculate and I remark about this. She is modest in response; she has done most of the work herself and feels that the tiled floor I am particularly praiseworthy of is not level and that next time around she may get someone in to do it!

Barbara took early retirement two years ago and the rooms that she lets for B&B were finished soon after then. She and her husband John bought the farmhouse and moved here some 20 years ago, but unfortunately John died ten years ago. Judging by the work that has been done since I got the sense that the house was a project that they both dreamed of and that Barbara has continued with that dream. Indeed the car she drives us back to Bellingham in was John's car bought earlier in the year that he died. Prior to leaving she fills our flasks with coffee and we settle the bill. Despite the wonderful surroundings it is far from being the most expensive B&B of the trip.

I ask about the whereabouts of a chemist to get one last pack of Compeed and Barbara directs us to it as she drops us off in the little square in the centre of town. After yesterdays experience Trevor has also reduced the weight of his rucksack and with Barbara's agreement has left some items with her, which he will arrange to pick up next week.

After buying another pack of Compeed, which, with what I still have in the rucksack, I am sure will see me through to the end of my journey; we go off in search of a bakery to get a sandwich for lunch. We set off up the road to leave Bellingham behind and once more rejoin the PW. Our early banter is very much about Boat Farm and the 'marvel' that Barbara appears to me to be.

I would certainly not need much of an excuse to stay at there again.

We leave the road and pick up a farm track to our left, which is quite a steep pull before we arrive at and go through the farm yard and out into a big field which is navigated by sighting marking posts and walking between them. It is still very grey and mizzley. We follow the narrative within the guide and the sign posts and arrive at a point where we are advised that we have an option of two routes; the main PW or an alternative route. I had discovered yesterday that for most of today's route I do not have an appropriate OS map, so the guide book is a key part of our navigational aids today. I am feeling rather self critical about the lack of an OS map as I purchased four in preparation for the walk, to supplement the four I already had and believed I had all parts of the route covered.

Given the mist and the poor conditions underfoot too, we decide to head for the alternative route as it basically follows the line of a wall and fence until both paths link up again. The path itself is virtually non existent though and the conditions underfoot are again very wet and boggy, but it is relatively easy to keep in touch with the wall. We cross a track at one point and encounter three men who are working in the wet conditions rebuilding a section of the wall. I greet them with a "nice day for walling" and they laugh, exchange greetings and then carry on with their task.

We arrive at the rejoining of both paths feeling very damp indeed. Now we head for a high point which has a cairn and PW signpost at Lough Shaw and from there seek and then head towards a second cairn and signpost at Lord's Shaw. All the time on this stretch, we keep getting glimpses through the swirling mist of the pepper pot cairn on the summit of Padon Hill. We will pass close to it later on in the morning.

The route, according to the guide appears to go right after climbing a stile in a wall; however the only discernable path clearly goes straight on. We follow it believing it may bear right shortly. It doesn't and gets less distinct before we emerge onto a track running at right angles from where we have come from. I work out from the limited section of map in the guide book where we are and we turn right and follow the track to a T junction with a B road.

We notice that the man and his teenage son that we met yesterday have gone left here, but I reckon we need to walk about 400 metres to our right to rejoin the main route. It turns out to be 450 metres before we arrive at a cattle grid, a PW sign and rejoin our route which now takes us along a clearer stony track that bypasses by about 400 metres the pepper pot summit cairn of Padon Hill.

There are conflicting stories about the provenance of the four and a half metre high pepper pot cairn. Some suggest it was constructed to commemorate the golden wedding anniversary of Sir Charles and Lady Morris-Bell of Otterburn Hall in either 1903 or 1913. It is suggested that it was built using stone from a chapel on the site that was previously erected by the Scottish Covenanting Minister, Alexander Peden and that the hill is named after him. Whatever the truth of the matter we decide that we are not going to try and climb a fence and find a route to let us have a closer inspection of it.

We continue down a steep slope to what the guide book describes as the "worst section of the PW". Before we get there we cross over a flagged area, where the flags are at least six inches below the water level in places. However when I dip my walking pole in either side of the submerged stones it goes down at least two feet, so we have no option but to stick to our underwater path.

We then start up a steep, boggy and rocky climb and shortly up this are met by three figures approaching in the opposite direction. Finding a 'passing place' is a bit tricky! The three figures turn out to be three Germans who are walking from Byrness to Bellingham (the reverse of our walk of today). They tell us it is very boggy for at least another two miles. In return for this helpful (if unwanted!) information, we tell them about the underwater path they will soon need to negotiate (touché). The climb up this steep hill is indeed a challenge but not as bad as a lot I have had to contend with over the past twelve days.

However I start to revise my perspective on the section as it now continues to follow a fence for about two miles over very wet and boggy ground until it leads down into the forest; which should provide relief at last we feel. Certainly not, there is no path and for the next mile the underfoot conditions are worse than ever as in addition to squelchy bogs and saturated ground there are also submerged tree routes to contend with.

Finally we reach a forest track and take fifteen minutes to rest and take on food and water by a gate. For me only the first three and a half miles across Sleightholme

Moor after leaving the Tan Hill Inn on Day Eight rank as a worse stretch of the PW in terms of challenging terrain. The last three miles have certainly been hellish though.

The mist has now cleared and we have emerging warm sunshine and views ahead of the vastness of Kielder forest. I can finally take off my over trousers and get some air to my legs. The sign next to the gate points back the way we have come and proclaims "Bellingham 9 ¾ miles". It is about 3pm (five and a half hours since we left the bakery in Bellingham). We are now on track; or so we think; for the rest of the day and have about six miles of walking through the forest till we get to Byrness.

After walking for about a mile along the track we hear a rumbling noise behind us and a lorry carrying a huge load of logs approaches. We stand aside to let it pass, however after travelling for about 400 metres it slows down again and stops and we soon catch up with it. The driver has got out of the cab and is looking under the lorry for something that he thinks may have dropped off. I never thought we would be able to claim we had overtaken a four ton truck. However the lorry is soon on its way again and for the second time we stand aside as it passes and eventually disappears into the distance.

We continue along the undulating track now in very pleasant sunshine until we finally arrive; just after Blakehopeburnhaugh; at a picnic spot where I have promised Trevor we will have a break.

Blakehopeburnhaugh's claim to fame, according to the guide book, is that it is allegedly the longest place name on the PW route. We spend a pleasant fifteen minutes resting tired and sore feet and aching limbs before we set off again and are soon directed off the main vehicular track and along a woodland path which takes us down to a river, where we encounter two frogs in quick succession.

Eventually we regain a clearer track and take a bridge over the river at Cottonshopeburn Foot. This sparks a debate between us as to whether this is not a longer place name than Blakehopeburnhaugh. We are interrupted in our dialogue and overtaken by a lady jogger coming up behind us. We can now see and hear at times traffic on the A68 road ahead and as we near the road arrive at a churchyard and are amazed to watch a deer cut left to right across it, dodging tombstones as it goes.

Once on the road we have no indication which way our B&B is. However Trevor has been building up the Byrness Hotel to me as somewhere he has had a good pint in the past and so we head right in order to call there to have a pint and to ask for directions to our night's accommodation. As we head up the drive to the Hotel we are greeted by a yapping Jack Russell and then a lady appears and tells us she is closing the Hotel, as she has to go and see her father in hospital tonight.

 She does tell us that we need to go on for about half a mile further north along the road to find our B&B, which turns out to be a row of terraced houses, which we are guided to access through a metal gate and a ginnel that opens out at the back of the property into a conservatory. We meet our hostess in the Conservatory area and are then shown to our room, requested to choose our evening meal; which we do; and get showered and changed.

Familiar faces greet us when we return downstairs; Trevor and Paul, Arthur (the young teenager) and his Dad and Con and Julia (the couple who stayed at Twice Brewed two nights ago and Bellingham last night and whose paths we have crossed several times since). We apologize to everyone for having to break the news that the 'pub' is closed this evening and are immediately reprimanded by our hostess, who informs us that we **are** staying at the 'pub'. The Byrness Hotel is apparently a guest House with three guest rooms. We are informed that the landlady there has ideas above her station. Firmly put in our place we are guided to the bar in the lounge and are delighted to discover that it boasts three hand-pulled Allandale beers; Golden Plover, Swift and Wolf; the latter being the strongest.

We all enjoy lots of PW stories and our meals, which are served in a dining room accessed by going out into the conservatory again and then back into the 'next house'. Later in the lounge the beer and the banter are flowing in equal measure and I am the only resident who is planning to do the whole walk to Kirk Yetholm in one day. There are two people staying who did the first 'half' today and were picked up by our landlady at 4.30pm and who will be dropped off there again tomorrow at about 9.30 to complete their walk to Kirk Yetholm.

Trevor, sensibly in my view, takes advantage of this opportunity and negotiates a lift in the morning to the half way point. It will mean a mile and a half climb up to the PW route where we can link up at Windy Gyle. This will mean he will only have another 15 miles to walk with me. I aim to be leaving at 6.30am at the latest and hope to link up with Trevor at around 12 to 12.30pm. This should ensure we are at the Border Hotel in Kirk Yetholm by around 7pm.

Con is the first to try a pint of Wolf and before the evening is out both Trevor's and Paul also try it. For my part I stick to the very pleasant, but less strong Golden Plover. If I am going to be up early and walk the 27 miles to Kirk Yetholm over the Cheviots I believe I may need a clear head. The landlord functions as our barman during the evening and both he and his wife join in at times with our conversation. We are all amazed at their story of what happened last week.

Apparently a lady PW walker was staying with them and was to be picked up at the half way point at half past four. She had apparently gone about three miles when, at about 9.45am, on a particularly waterlogged section she had slipped into and up to her armpits in a bog. She had managed to text her husband who was at home and avail him of this information, before she had managed to haul herself out, with the aid of the two walking poles she was using.

Having been submerged in the bog her phone now ceased to function, but instead of backtracking and taking steps to let him know she was ok, she carried on with her walk.

Meanwhile a frantic husband had been in touch with the police and mountain rescue and before long three separate rescue teams were out looking for her. It wasn't until about 3.30pm when she was approaching Windy Gyle to begin her descent to the 'meeting point' that she was 'found' by one of the search teams; who enquired whether she was the lady who had been stuck in a bog and who had text her husband to tell him that. She seemed very surprised that people would be out looking for her and even later when she was back at the B&B she still couldn't understand what all the fuss was about.

I leave the lounge to go up to bed at about ten past ten, with everyone else still intent on enjoying a little more beer and convivial banter. My feet have held up well today and I decide to re-compeed them in the morning. I get out the stuff I will wear tomorrow and pack the rucksack ready for an early start.

Although I wake briefly twice during the night I do have a good sleep until about 5.20am. I decide to get up then rather than wait for my 5.45am alarm call and get ready for my early start.

I have negotiated with the landlady to leave out some cereal for my breakfast and for a pack lunch to be available too. The cereal turns out to be Fruit and Fibre. I make a cup of tea and pack the lunch into the rucksack and retrieve my boots from the drying room and am on my way by five past six.

DISTANCE WALKED TODAY: 16 MILES

TOTAL DISTANCE WALKED: 246 MILES

CHAPTER SIXTEEN

BYRNESS TO KIRK YETHOLM (Wednesday 25th July)

"Hi all, Glorious last day, sunshine, wonderful scenery. Started at 6am this morning, arrived at 6.15 this evening. On my own for the first half, Trevor rejoined me for last leg. Peter"

"Hi Sandra, The eagle has landed. Am in god's own country. Just having a welcome pint. Peter"

I head off in dampish conditions following overnight rain and after leaving the B&B head back along the road towards the Byrness Hotel (or Guest House). However I cross the road before reaching it and pick up the PW, which heads up along a path, with overhanging trees and grasses for company. It isn't long therefore before I am donning my over-trousers as I am getting soaked by the undergrowth that spills out onto the path. The first stretch up to Byrness Pike is initially through a forested area and is a steep and scrambly ascent, but I enjoy it.

At the summit I pause and reflect a while on my surroundings, I am alone in the hills and am feeling good. I pick up the path from Byrness Pike and head on, knowing I will remain on high ground for most of the day now. I have to negotiate several boggy areas;

including one I imagine to be the place where a week ago our lady was momentarily stuck up to her armpits. It seems to take ages to get to the summit of Ravens Knowe (527m).

I pick up some speed over some flag-stoned areas and see my second buzzard of the week circling over Houx Hill. I am flummoxed for a while by a sign that gives me an alternative route to Windy Gyle; where Trevor is going to meet me later. The main route indicates 'Windy Gyle 8 ½ miles', the alternative proclaims, 'Windy Gyle 8m', but there is no reference to an alternative route in the guide book, neither is there an alternative route marked on the OS map. I decide therefore to stick to the main route. This drops down for a while before rising gently and following the contours of the land round the shoulder of a hill, which eventually brings me to the Yearning Saddle Hut. This is a purpose built mountain refuge and I rest awhile there and fill in the visitor book and eat a banana before heading on.

I am now minus both over-trousers and cagoule as the sun is out and the day is really pleasantly warm. Again I find sections of flagstones interspersed with more challenging terrain, but continue to make good progress over both Lamb Hill (511m) and Beefstand Hill (562m), and then drop down before the final steep path that takes me over Mozie Law (552m) and up on to Windy

Gyle (619m), where Trevor is waiting for me. There is a large rambling pile of rocks for a summit cairn, as well as a Trig point and Trevor has been here for an hour and twenty minutes. He was dropped off about 1 ½ miles below at Trowes and had a steep pull up to the summit. It is 11.45 am when I arrive and I am pleased that after the earlier slow progress, I get there ahead of my predicted arrival time of 12noon. I have covered the 13 miles from Byrness in about 5 ½ hours.

We decide to have lunch before moving on, which for me provides a welcome break too. Just beyond the summit is a signpost which states; '7m to The Schill'. The Schill is the last summit of the day (indeed of the whole PW) and is about half way to Kirk Yetholm. However, before that there is firstly a long pull up to Kings' Seat (531), which is just a trig point in the middle of nowhere.

However the real slog proves to be the ascent to Cairn Hill, which marks a split of ridges; one running on to The Cheviot and the other turning sharp left to Auchope Cairn. Trevor finds this long steep climb quite challenging and is very relieved to arrive at the gentler sloping ground near the summit (777m). The climb has its lighter moments too though as Trevor spots a grass snake, about 18 inches long as it slithers across the path ahead.

We take a well earned break at Cairn Hill and decide against adding a further 1 ½ miles to our journey by going up to and back to the summit of The Cheviot itself. Although I might have done this if on my own I recognise that arriving at Kirk Yetholm with Trevor early enough (and in a fit state) to enjoy the evening and the glow of satisfaction from completing the whole journey, is more important. After all at 815m it would only be the fourth highest peak of my PW journey.

A long track of duck board; a new underfoot experience; eases our passage to Auchope Cairn (725m) where two huge cairns about fifty metres apart dominate the rocky summit. We take some shelter from the wind; which seems to have changed to a north easterly again; for the first time since Day Two of my walk and seems to be gathering in strength too.

We then inch down the steep slope at the other side of the summit and work our way to a second mountain refuge hut. Trevor finds this descent even more of a challenge than the ascent of Cairn Hill and I have time to stop and take a picture of some cows; which are safely on the other side of a barbed wire fence. It somehow seems appropriate to have a picture of some cows after the number of times they have played a part in my journey.

The refuge hut provides an opportunity for a tea break and I leave some provisions that I will now no longer need and sign the visitor's book. Soon after leaving the shelter of the hut, a lizard runs across our path and the roll call of fauna that have shared my journey is further increased.

Although the pull up to The Schill is severe it is only about 600 metres of a climb and as such not as challenging as the ascent of Cairn Hill. I am really enjoying today, I am summiting tops, I am ridge walking, I am nearing the end of my epic walk and the sun is shining and in Trevor I will have someone to share a pint with at the end of the day. I have had the morning walking on my own and now have company again – a perfect metaphor for the walk as a whole.

I clamber up to the summit cairn of The Schill (601m) before rejoining Trevor and we both head down from what should be and is the last summit of the day and the walk. After about half an hour we arrive at a dip in the descent that allows us to choose whether to take the higher or lower level route and choose the latter. A sign post tells us that it is 4 ½ miles to Kirk Yetholm. A pleasant two hours follows in which I start to feel sad at the prospect of leaving my friend (the PW) tomorrow. We see lots of horses in jackets, some without and even a donkey in a field with less than a mile to go to our destination.

We are now on a tarmac road and have a steep climb to negotiate, which even has benches on the side in places for weary walkers to rest if they need to. We arrive at The Border Hotel and take a picture and Trevor goes inside to get in the beer. 'Holy Cow' bitter – well it seems very appropriate somehow and it certainly goes down well. I send off messages and texts to tell all that 'the eagle has landed' and we go in to register and are taken to our room. The en-suite has a bath – wonderful! I am soon clean and changed and ready to go down for another pint and a meal – we have booked a table for 8.30pm. However before then I make sure I get my certificate signed and I write an entry in the book, which is kept there for all PW walkers to record the date and time and a comment about their journey.

We have a very enjoyable meal and whilst doing so down another two pints of Holy Cow. Afterwards I have the malt I promised myself and resisted earlier in the week to round off the evening, before tiredness sets in and so it's off to bed.

DISTANCE WALKED TODAY: 27 MILES

TOTAL DISTANCE WALKED: 273 MILES

CHAPTER SEVENTEEN

KIRK YETHOLM TO HOME (Thursday 26th July) and SOME FINAL REFLECTIONS

I sleep well and it feels strange waking up and not getting ready to head off on another day's walk. It is also unusual not to need to be rushing down to breakfast either. Today I can and do have a 'full scottish' as opposed to a 'full english'. I had planned my return home journey well in advance, in order to ensure I would be back home in time to undertake a couple of errands that would take several hours to complete. The journey would have involved catching a bus from Kirk Yetholm at 9.20am and heading to Kelso. Here I would board a second bus and travel to a roundabout on the A6901, before boarding a third bus from the other side of the roundabout to Berwick-upon-Tweed Railway station. I would arrive there at 12.26pm and then catch a train to Leeds that was due to depart at 12.47.

I had suggested to Trevor that we could share the journey and that he could get off the train at Newcastle, in order for him to get back to Whitley Bay. However Trevor had arranged for his son Rob to come and pick us up at about 11am and agreed that Rob would drop me off at Berwick station in plenty of time for my train. We paid the bill and I also paid for two pints for Paul and Trevor; who I knew were booked into the restaurant for a meal at 7.30pm this evening. We then went to sit and wait on a picnic bench outside the Hotel for Rob to arrive. Just as Trevor predicted he arrived well before 11am and it wasn't long before we were negotiating country lanes and within about 10 minutes leaving Scotland behind and re-entering Northumberland.

I had over an hour to spare at Berwick before my train and bought a paper to read to catch up on what was going on in the world. The build up to the Olympics in London seemed to dominate and as I had tickets for two events to look forward to, was also of interest to me. During the journey to Leeds I also lunched on some of my remaining provisions and started to get my head around the fact that my Pennine Way Odyssey was finally at an end.

It had been a really enjoyable experience on the whole, albeit with the occasional trial or tribulation to overcome. I had walked over some amazing countryside and witnessed some wonderful scenery. I had experienced, or so it seemed, most of the fauna of the area first hand, in one way or another, been attacked by a cow, dive bombed by a lapwing, edged past llamas and horses, seen loads of rabbits and sheep, a hare, a snake and a lizard. I had been sung to by oyster-catchers, snipes, curlews, lapwings, blackbirds, thrushes, skylarks and many more besides.

I met a number of people all undertaking their own PW journeys, and no doubt with their own stories to tell, but I had enjoyed the overlaps between their stories and my own, indeed some had become very much a part of my journey too. The opportunity to share parts of my journey with people I knew before it started and will frequently meet again, also worked well. I can imagine on future occasions reliving the parts of the journey we each shared together.

I hadn't too long to wait before my connection at Leeds, which was going to Skipton. This meant that I could get off at Saltaire and then walk the mile or so back home and be there by 4pm. Once at home I emptied my rucksack and sorted out things that needed washing and discovered in a side pocket the feather I had stashed there last Sunday. I had forgotten all about it, at least there would be a tangible memento of the walk to present to Sandra, when I picked her up from her travels tomorrow. Apart from the two pairs of walking shorts I had used all the clothing I had taken on at least one occasion, which I felt good about. Within my provisions stash, I still had three snack packs of apricots, two packets of yoghurt coated raisins and an energy bar.

After a quick cup of tea, I loaded a two seater settee into the back of my car. I had collected it from a friend of my daughters' before setting off on my journey, so knew that it would just fit. I then set off to visit my sister over the other side of the Pennines, to deliver this to her. In doing so I passed the B&B I had stayed in at the end of the fourth day of my PW journey; and that seemed a long time ago now.

After visiting my sister I carried on a further six miles to my brother-in law's to collect Maisy, our cocker spaniel. I had taken her there with Sandra on the morning of the third day of the journey; the day after I had walked for over 12 hours and covered 32 miles. I travelled back across the M62 and at its high point under the bridge that carries the PW over it and that I had walked across on that day too. For some reason some of the events of that day seemed clearer and nearer to me than many subsequent days. I wonder why!

The End

N.B. All the distances referred to in the book are based on a combination of distances given within the Guidebook I used (See below) and my own calculations from where I had to, or did deviate from the route; for example in getting to and from accommodation off route at the beginning or end of a day.

GUIDE BOOKS AND MAPS USED:

1. The Pennine Way; A Cicerone Guide by Paddy Dillon Third Edition 2010
2. The Cleveland Way: Official National Trail Guide by Ian Sampson Revised Edition 2010
3. OS Map OL1 The Peak District
4. OS Map OL21 South Pennines
5. OS Map OL2 Yorkshire Dales – Southern and Western areas
6. OS Map OL30 Yorkshire Dales – Northern and Central areas
7. OS Map OL19 Howgill Fells and Upper Eden Valley
8. OS Map OL31 North Pennines – Teesdale and Weardale
9. OS Map OL43 Hadrian's Wall – Haltwhistle and Hexham
10. OS Map OL16 The Cheviot Hills – Jedburgh and Wooler

PLACES I STAYED IN DURING MY PENNINE WAY JOURNEY

1. **Campsite:The eve of my journey: Upper Booth Farm**
   (There are lots of options in and around Edale itself. Given my commitment to stay a number of nights under canvas and the fact it was about a mile into but on the route, it suited me to stay here)
2. **At the end of Day One: Old House B&B, Torside, Glossop**
   (There are a number of B&Bs in Crowden- about a mile further on and a camping barn too, but the Old House was the first call I made and they had a vacancy)
3. **At the end of Day Two: Home!**
   (I had planned to wild camp somewhere between Standedge and the M62, but the continuous rain led to the emergence of a Plan B – I think I may well have looked to book a B&B in or around Mankinholes if I was tackling this stretch again – A long day but this may then give me an option of walking to Cowling on the following day)
4. **At the end of Day Three: Badger Fields Farm, Blackshaw Head**
   (When I was trying to book accommodation in Hebden Bridge, I had really struggled because of a literature festival that happened to be on at the same time. Badger Fields Farm is two miles through Callis Bridge and almost on the Pennine Way)
5. **At the end of Day Four: Winterhouse Barn, Cowling**
   (This is only 100 metres from where the PW crosses the A6068 and as such was a perfect place to stay. There are a few other B&Bs in Cowling. The only evening meal

option nearby was a Curry House – not a problem for me!)

6. **At the end of Day Six: Wild camping above Malham Tarn**
(The evening leg from Malham to the place I camped at was necessary for me to shorten the following day as I was heading to Hawes. There are plenty of B&B and camping options at Malham and staying at Malham could provide an opportunity for the following day to be split into two, staying at Horton-in- Ribblesdale at the end of the first day)

7. **At the end of Day Seven: Bulls Head Hotel, Hawes**
(This is not a pub, as I imagined, but there are plenty in Hawes. There are also plenty of B&Bs to choose from too)

8. **At the end of Day Eight: Tan Hill Inn, Tan Hill**
(Whilst I may have my criticisms of Tan Hill for its accommodation, the food and beer were good and for me it was a must to stay here. It marks the half way mark of the PW. It was the first 'nail in the wall' of my pre-planned itinerary)

9. **At the end of Day Nine: Belvedere House B&B, Middleton-in-Teesdale**
(Middleton has a range of Hotels and B&Bs to choose from. The Belvedere suited me fine, as did it's proximity to the Hotel nest door! There are however lots of places to eat out in Middleton)

10. **At the end of Day Ten: The Post Office, Garrigill**
(The original plan had been to wild camp near Alston, but as it turned out The Post Office added much to my

overall experience. It's proximity to the pub was also a plus)

11. **At the end of Day Eleven: Twice Brewed Inn, Twice Brewed**
(This was always a good place to link up with Trevor and despite being about half a mile away from the PW, is in a good position to ensure the remainder of the walk can be done in three days. There are other options at Once Brewed, Greenhead or Housesteads)

12. **At the end of Day Twelve: Boat Farm B&B, Bellingham**
(I had originally booked a B&B in Bellingham itself, but they could not accommodate Trevor too. Trevor had found the 'gem' that is Boat Farm. The down side is that it is a mile out of Bellingham. There are a number of B&Bs in the town itself)

13. **At the end of Day Thirteen: Forest View B&B, Byrness**
(Another excellent if accidental find! Accommodation in Byrness is limited, so if you want somewhere that offers a comfortable bed, ok facilities, a choice of hot meal and a lounge with a bar that offers at least three cask beers, then this is not a bad place to stop)

14. **At the end of Day Fourteen: The Border Hotel, Kirk Yetholm**
(Again, whilst there are a range of options in terms of where to stay in Kirk Yetholm, I particularly wanted to stay at the Border Hotel, because of its significance as being 'the end of the Way' and the place where Wainwright left money to give a free pint to all those who completed the whole route from Edale)

SUMMITS (400m plus) - VISITED DURING MY JOURNEY

NAME OF SUMMIT	HEIGHT	DAY	CHAPTER
Cross Fell	893m	10	Twelve
Great Dunn Fell	848	10	Twelve
Little Dunn Fell	842	10	Twelve
Knock Fell	794	10	Twelve
Cairn Hill	743	14	Sixteen
Auchope Cairn	726	14	Sixteen
Great Shunner Fell	716	7	Nine
Pen-y-ghent	694	6	Eight
Fountains Fell	662	6	Eight
Narrowgate Beacon (High Cup Nick)	656	9	Eleven
Kinder Low	633	1	Three
Bleaklow Head	633	1	Three
Ravens Knowe	627	14	Sixteen
Windy Gyle	619	14	Sixteen
Pikeman Hill	616	10	Twelve
The Schil	601	14	Sixteen
Rasp Hill	590	9	Eleven
Black Hill	582	2	Four
Sandy Heys	575	1	Three
Beefstand Hill	552	14	Sixteen
Mozie Law	552	14	Sixteen
Mill Hill	544	1	Three
Kings Seat	531	14	Sixteen
Ogre Hill	516	14	Sixteen
Lamb Hill	7511	14	Sixteen
Ashop Head	510	1	Three
Windy Crag	491	14	Sixteen
Blackstone Edge	472	2	Four
White Hill	466	2	Four
Withins Height	450	5	Seven
Wolf Stones	443	5	Seven
Race Yate	427	7	Nine
Byrness Hill	414	14	Sixteen
Stoodley Pike	400	2	Four

The Author at the end of Day One of the walk

Peter was born in 1950 in Lancashire and grew up and went to school in Horwich, near Bolton. He has lived in Yorkshire for the past 25 years. He had a forty year career in Local Government, before retiring in 2009. Peter is married, to Sandra and has two daughters; Becky and Jenny and a granddaughter Bella.

He has always had a love affair with fell walking and the Lake District in particular and during his forties visited all the 2000 foot summits of the Lakeland Fells. He took up running aged 49 and since then has completed 12 marathons. Completing the Pennine Way has been a long held ambition.